a blossom shrouds me, the breeze follows my funeral

mpT
MODERN POETRY IN TRANSLATION
The best of world poetry

No.2 2017
© Modern Poetry in Translation 2017 and contributors

ISSN (print) 0969-3572
ISSN (online) 2052-3017
ISBN (print) 978-1-910485-17-0
ISBN (ebook) 978-1-910485-18-7

Editor: Sasha Dugdale
Managing Editor: Deborah de Kock
Development Manager: Sarah Hesketh
Web and Communications Manager: Ed Cottrell
Design by Jenny Flynn
Cover art by Walid El-Masri

Printed and bound in Great Britain by Charlesworth Press, Wakefield
For submissions and subscriptions please visit www.mptmagazine.com

Modern Poetry in Translation Limited. A Company Limited by Guarantee
Registered in England and Wales, Number 5881603
UK Registered Charity Number 1118223

Supported using public funding by

ARTS COUNCIL ENGLAND

Golan Haji's work in this issue is a commission by Shubbak in partnership
with the British Council.

شباك: نافذة على الثقافة العربية المعاصرة

A WINDOW ON CONTEMPORARY ARAB CULTURE

SHUBBAK

MODERN POETRY IN TRANSLATION

A Blossom Shroud

CONTENTS

Focus

Reviews

EDITORIAL

Mona Kareem, activist, translator and poet, talks in this issue about
her translations of Ashraf Fayadh's *Instructions Within* (pp.102–108).
Fayadh was imprisoned in Saudia Arabia and sentenced to death for
apostasy on the evidence of this collection. Mona notes the collective
spirit of the translation and how it brought with it companionship, a
'secret love' which bound Fayadh's translators together in the face of
monstrosity. Marilyn Hacker, the translator of Syrian activist and
exile Fadwa Souleiman, writes in a similar way (p.114) about the act of
friendship and reciprocity that is translation: 'I worked with [Fadwa]
learning to recite Arabic poetry, Darwish especially, the way she had
in drama school in Damascus'. Stephen Watts has often talked about
translation as a poetic and creative act, but he has also written about
the loving solidarity which he experiences as a translator and which
infuses his translations. For the sequence published here Stephen
visited Golan Haji in Paris and they worked on the poems in Golan's
flat whilst Golan's baby daughter slept.

Translating someone's work means listening to them so intently
you can hear their pulse, you can hear them pausing to swallow. You
follow their thoughts deep into the subconscious and you find there a
synthesis of your own subconscious and theirs. Although translation
is often described as the closest act of reading, it is also an act of
enormous sympathy between the poet and the translator. A poem is a
projection in words of something shapeless and nameless: an instinct
or a sensation, a memory or a yearning, and to translate that requires
us to reach through the net of words stretched out on the page to
a place beyond. If we do not ourselves attempt to befriend that
initial impulse it is hard to translate the poem. We are reduced to
marshalling words into a harmonious but unimportant order.

I am not for a moment advocating carelessness towards the actual
words of a poem. They are the coordinates, the map, the hand
gestures, all we have to go on. Nor is this any kind of theoretical guide

I am bound to
want to make the
poem live in my
own tongue, in
my own mouth

The very first issue of *Modern Poetry in Translation* is
now online at www.modernpoetryintranslation.com

to translation. The expression of sympathy is an individual matter: I only know that when my sympathy is engaged I am bound to want to make the poem live in my own tongue, in my own mouth. I am changed by it.

Most of the general debate around poetry translation is occupied with the notion of failure, or even worse, with the destruction of an original. We don't think of friendship in this way. It is possible to love a friend and know their love without the relationship being destructive or somehow failing. This is not a utopian thought.

The best friendships allow insights on both sides, they 'change without perishing'. In the same way translation is a dynamic practice. Mona is right when she says in her conversation with Alice Guthrie that the old clichés about 'bridge' and 'exchange' are useless because they imply stasis and distance: two rocky islands with a cautious footbridge between them. We should instead be talking about how translation changes us, how poet and translator are no longer who they were, and the poem is no longer what it once was – it has undergone the closest act of friendship.

Sasha Dugdale

RAINER MARIA RILKE

Translated by Paul Batchelor

In 1922 Rainer Maria Rilke famously completed the *Duino Elegies* within a few weeks, after a ten-year period in which progress on the great work had been very slow. Rilke being Rilke, he had produced dozens of other astonishing poems during this time, but he was rather dismissive towards them and didn't bother publishing them. Simultaneously, he produced a second masterpiece: the *Sonnets to Orpheus*. He had four years left. In those four years he wrote hundreds of poems in German and nearly 450 in French – and this at a time when his health, never very good, was steadily deteriorating. The question of why Rilke began writing in French at this time has attracted much speculation. Reading Paul Valéry's 'Le Cimetière marin' seems to have been one of the things that helped Rilke unlock the *Duino Elegies*, and he set to work translating it into German, so perhaps he found his French voice while doing so. Rilke's French poems are far less emotionally intense than his work in German, and they have a settled, rustic, light, placid feel to them that reflects how he was living at the time (he wrote them at the chateau at Muzot where he lived from February 1921 until his death: Muzot was the closest he ever came to having a home). Rilke was aware that his French poems were work of secondary intensity – he likened writing the sequences 'Les Roses' and the 'Valaisian Quatrains' to 'baking a little cake' and said that writing in French was not like 'work' at all – but he seems to have had a little more regard for the sequence he published (in what we'd call a limited edition) as *Vergers*. Here, I have translated the title sequence of that collection, 'Orchard'.

Orchard

I

And why else, borrowed tongue,
why else did I dare speak a word
of you, if not to say orchard –
the country name that haunted me so long?

Fenced-in with detail, or shipwrecked
in the abstract?
Pity the poet whose song
would capture all the promise of that name!

It is the privilege of the lyre
to voice you: orchard.
Name that breathes & listens, name
to lure honeybees, name without peer

whose dazzle hides ancient springs –
full & invisible,
syllable against syllable
you overflow, you redouble everything.

II

Around which star does all
our ponderous yearning
spin? Where are the heavens
of our promised zeal?

Or do we sway together
simply to please each other?
Let us tread
lightly that we may feel the planet turning
according to this force, according to that force...

Look again at the orchard:
weighed-down – of course, of course –
but in that heaviness
you can taste summer's happiness.

III

Never was land more real
than in your branches; never was gold
more weightless than in the lace
your shadows throw on the grass.

This is our inheritance.
All that is heavy, all that must be sated, will reveal
that the path of tenderness
is endless...

A silent fountain dozes at your still
centre: once
she could solve any riddle;
now she leaves them untold.

IV

The gods we abandoned –
how did they hide their grace? Where did it go?
Gifted children who couldn't outgrow
their provincial roots...

Behind a veil of sound
beetles & bees
circle the fruits –
heavenly labours!

Those long-forgotten gods, lost in the past,
will never altogether disappear:
they will be here
when we meet our accusers face to face at last.

V

What memory, what hope
      can you conjure, my orchard?
You, the nibbling sheep;
      I, the good shepherd...

It's Sunday – my day off,
      though your work is far from over.
I think I could gaze up
      through your branches forever...

To be a shepherd: a fine life!
      And won't my peacefulness deepen
your apples' flavour as they ripen,
      now that you know I'll leave?

VI

The orchard, like a summer dress let fall
from your shoulders... didn't you feel
the consolation of sweet
grass under your feet?

No coronation, no victory parade:
it impressed you simply by becoming great.
An hour slipped away, and that was that.
You waited,

a book for company, implicated
in the myriad
shadows that mirrored
a play of symbols – impossible to read.

VII

Orchard, content to coax each apple
to its potential – how well they know
your age-old instincts, your supple
responses to their come-and-go...

What success, what order you achieve! They grow
insistent in the twisted branches
until, delighted with their strength, they overflow
in the still air...

Your dangers, my dangers –
are they not all one?
O my orchard, O my twin!
The same wind compels us to be gentle, to be severe.

MERCEDES CEBRIÁN

Translated by Terence Dooley

In 'Floating Population' Mercedes Cebrián sets out to speak for and of her generation, with great irony and indirection. Hers is the first generation to grow up out of the shadow of Franco's dictatorship, under a new and initially uncertain Spanish democracy built on an agreed silence about where the bodies were buried. They know new freedoms and a new plenty, and become adult as enthusiastic citizens of Europe, where for so long Spain was the outcast and rogue nation. They have 'self-belief': 'We're ok, that's our motto for now.' But this confidence rests on a new conformity, a bland consumerism, and hides unease and confusion. Can this ok-ness of what might seem in retrospect a golden age, really last, or does it contain the seeds of its own destruction? 'Someone is filming now | the documentary of all that certainty?'

The book, *Common Market,* which ends with this poem, was published in 2006. Six years later Mercedes wrote in the introduction to the Argentinian edition that she never imagined how soon the half-anticipated disasters would begin to strike, as she described the apathy and helpless complacency of her peers. The Atocha atrocity had already taken place, and we see echoes of that in the poem. Financial catastrophe was round the corner: 'Are there fewer bubbles now | or am I imagining it?' Well, no, the bubbles burst, and all that was left were the broken bottles after the party.

Mercedes takes up the story again in *Malgastar/Squandering* (2016), chosen as an *El País* Book of the Year. She is a matchless social commentator and wit, but also a deeply personal lyric poet. There is nobody like her, in Spain or elsewhere.

Floating Population

1

All right: the maids, who help themselves
to our scent, to our best clothes,
these we dismiss, without a thought,
but what we feel, what we feel at the core
is the very opposite of that spear-thrust.
Scissors far outclass us, flourishing their jaws.

We were badly cut, the taxidermist also
allowed us too much freedom, and we move
through cities lit up with our own wattage's
unasked-for light. Water we couldn't reproduce.
We undergo diasporas, the likeness of diasporas,
we undergo laborious attempts at speech,
all our effort pours into our voice,
we advance, we attack, we jib at no,
we can't bear silence.

                         Whether we look
ahead or to one side, makes no difference,
speech is a vortex, the pain we feel
at what we said this afternoon, for example,
is also a vortex. So the voice persists,
alters, emits, and seeks a presence.
And, meanwhile, what do we have to give
each other but a pair of knives
whose fearful blades are too light to draw blood.

Mercedes Cebrián © Sheila Melham

2

We could have been glossed as broadly lucky,
our lives were caressed by a kind of ease.

   we even called our parents by their names

Civil partnerships were established, so was
self-belief: the climate they gave us
is a reality now.

The future is white now
and processed, like our supper,
so you don't need teeth to chew it
as once you did.
The great noise when it comes will sound
as grim as chard, Ceuta and Melilla
will be gone, we'll stroll
through withered parks, called after
ex-ministers. No magnifying-glass
remains. There
we'll be smashed to shards
(the shard recalls
an ancient wholeness). There
the vertical silhouette of the rocket
won't be aimed at the moon
(rocket too sounds to us
so dated now).

The floating population won't decide.
It doesn't know who
is caressing it, helplessness
reaches it in the form
of corporate benevolence.
Things suit us: this is the jargon.
What we've swallowed is the happy medium,
like the fillet steak they gave us,
not in vain were we able to metabolise.

> on our first flight
> they showed us the pilot's cabin

Patience
explodes in our hands. We weren't invited
to the memorial; we'll have been here
such ages, relieved not to have lost
all movement in our legs. We'll
have been as well-acquainted with democracy
as with olive oil. Someone is filming now
the documentary of all that certainty.

3

To control the oilfields
now that our hands are free
to write in lower case
to make the minimum of fuss
to end an era, knowing
we end it since it wasn't us
who christened it 'an era'.

To be lock-keepers,
To repatriate
excessive emotion
to save it for our pets.
The worms by now are experts
on our anatomy, we must
go to them for advice.
Nonetheless, there remain
textures we might touch:
foam perhaps
though not sandpaper.
Our hands know this.

We mustn't get distracted,
to set up one's encampment
in debate is a mistake
and one day we'll pay for it
with a picnic in the desert.
Today we celebrate
the end of multiplicity.
This is what it was all about:
splinters
empty bottles after the party
recyclable glass.
It's the supremacy
of prime numbers
it's a stuck zip
it's chickpeas put to soak
to no identifiable purpose.
Are there fewer bubbles now

or am I imagining it?
I can no longer scrawl
my signature where they point,
nor make any plans, nor even
lengthen
a list.

ANJA KAMPMANN

Translated by Anne Posten

Anja Kampmann's poems address on the first level sensual experience: of landscapes and images, as is suggested by the title of her first poetry collection *Proben von Stein und Licht* (Samples of Stone and Light), Carl Hanser Verlag, 2016). Yet even this simple title gives a hint into the layered use of language that gives her work both depth and playfulness. *Proben* are samples, but the word also suggests rehearsal, attempt – an approach to images and themes that remains open rather than definitive. In Kampmann's poems musicality is paramount. The poems are personal in the sense that they are derived from lived experience of place, yet Kampmann uses precise language and relies on rhythm to lend her images power, thereby distancing herself from the text and allowing structure and sound to be the primary carriers of meaning. Nor are the landscapes in these poems simply sites of natural beauty; rather, they are often occasions to reflect on history and concrete contemporary issues.

The tension between precision and openness, and the emphasis on sound, make these poems a challenge, but also a great joy to translate. I worked closely with the author to find rhythms and sounds that held a similar power in English, even if they differed from those in the original. Also particularly important in the translation was the preservation of the multiplicity of relationships between words: Kampmann's poems are often sparsely punctuated, allowing for various syntactical readings and a pace that drives forward while also stretching back, drawing the reader into the poem's own space and time.

a landscape that lies there...

a landscape that lies there
as if waiting for a tide

to breathe some life into it
who reads the wind over the plains

all the tortuous old stories
sketch themselves in the sky

just as contour just as line of winter
saying nothing no one thinks

the towns are to blame
as they flatten themselves against the horizon

what is it (say the clouds) that keeps you?

the crooked back of the world
has long peered into space

and at night with polished lenses
they measure

the distance to night
is small

in the songs an unquiet moon waits
for day what is it that it sees here

history of ploughlines

the love of a house
where we shall be warm

amber

manoeuvres on the Baltic
the light as if keeping beneath the soundwaves of shots
held as a test to the cold temples of this sky

it's not that
this airspace would ever forget its towns
storks come
you see the images of these guns in their barrels
the future mutters to itself

it's only plums
hanging dried and black between the blossoms
black moths tricks of the light

or the trenches around the fields,
now aimed.

his flight does not lie in anatomy...

his flight does not lie in anatomy
between feathers and lighter bones
you sense a point where poplars
touch the sky what are swallows
a summer day long on the hill beg tal
the uneasy wheat fieldbloom between
the stalks your seat of audible wind
it is day I keep night within would
never forget more than now will
there be a day when this rustling
of trees is missing ah bird who in his wheel
carries riddles written by the land
unrecognized it stretches before you planes
a few more plants and I as border dream
that I can no longer tell
the fields apart.

of kaliningrad you kept...

of kaliningrad you kept
the semolina pudding the tin pot in the morning
at boarding school the dogs the wild ones with broken
tails and finally a ship
that came toward you distant and far later
in the harbour the shadows of caps broke
the view broke behind collars
the weeks out between war and marine

lay miles up sea and halls so narrow
and potatoes so many and only
the screeching of gulls.

globe

and no one knows how deep the lake is
over which you swim pyramids
of knowledge and far above the stars
softly shifting their answers but
on the shore someone stands and waits
with a simple cloth in which the grass
still clings this day
in the dark it has the colours of
your skin but in these skies
missiles are once more steered by warmth but
the thing with the cold sea concerns
no one. the borders lick
their wounds almost silently in the sand
but in the dark someone stands
and waits till you come.

SHEN HAOBO

Translated by Liang Yujing

Shen Haobo, born in 1976, is considered one of the most controversial voices among the new generation of Chinese poets for being both wickedly erotic and politically satirical in his poetry. In 1998, as an undergraduate, he shocked poetry circles with a fierce article 'Who Made a Fool of the Nineties?', criticising the mainstream poetic trend in the 1990s. By 2000 he was known as the leading poet of the 'Lower Body Group', a poetry group characterised by its erotic writing, which brought him both fame and infamy. Apart from eroticism, politics is the other indispensable element of his poetry. His first collection *Great Evil in the Heart* (2004) was banned and he went abroad for a few months to escape arrest. Shen is not a real dissident but his poetry always has a rebellious temperament. His early poems are explicit and edgy, while his later poems have become more profound, especially after he encountered the trouble brought by his work. He is also one of the most successful publishers whose company Xiron has produced more bestsellers than any other in China. A rebellious poet and shrewd businessman, Shen Haobo is such a complex figure on the Chinese poetry scene that we might be tempted to fall back to his own words: a poet with 'great evil in the heart'.

The poems here are taken from 'Wenlou Village Accounts', a sequence of seven poems written by Shen Haobo after his visit to the village in the early 2000s. Wenlou Village is one of China's AIDS villages, due to a 1991–1995 plasmapheresis campaign by the Henan provincial government, known as the Plasma Economy, in which blood plasma was extracted in exchange for money. The campaign attracted three million donors and subsequently about 40% of them contracted AIDS. According to official statistics, there are 38 such villages in Henan Province. Tomb-Sweeping Day, also known as the Chingming Festival in China, falls on 4 or 5 April each year and is a holiday when people visit the family graves to commemorate and pray to their ancestors.

Ma Heling In Fact

In fact she's a person waiting for death
the way hundreds of people do in this village.
In fact her husband is one already dead
just like all the other dead persons in this village.
In fact she hasn't reconciled herself to dying in that way.
In fact she remarried less than a year after her husband's death.
In fact the man who married her also had a newly dead wife.
In fact Ma Heling, now in her fifties,
still looks plump and handsome.
In fact she's got AIDS that has started to affect her.
In fact there are hundreds of people waiting for death like her.
In fact the man who married her was a normal healthy guy.
In fact this guy had no choice but to marry an AIDS victim
if he still wanted a woman.
In fact it's impossible for any healthy woman to marry
a man whose wife has just died of AIDS.
In fact death has settled down in this village,
collecting people without even giving notice.
In fact the village is done for, dying out.
In fact they are still alive.
In fact they have to live until they die.
In fact they have to do some living things before their death.
In fact the man who married her really wanted to marry her,
for he, in his prime, needed a woman; even though she,
in fact useless, could only sit there or
walk slowly with her hands tucked in her sleeves,
he still wanted to marry her.
In fact this woman can still spread her legs in bed.
In fact this woman still has plenty of flesh.

He does wish she'd never die so that every night
there would be a living woman lying in his bed.
In fact the village distributes condoms to every family.
In fact the man who married her never uses condoms.
In fact she once asked, *Aren't you afraid of getting infected Aren't you*
afraid of death?
In fact he is afraid of death,
while in fact he still doesn't use condoms,
doesn't think he'll be so unfortunate, in fact in their village
almost all the men of his age have been unfortunate
but in fact they got infected by selling blood, in fact
the man who married her has never heard of anyone falling ill by
        fucking his wife.
In fact, to a peasant, fucking one's wife with a rubber sheath –
that sounds in fact more fucking incredible than death.

Cheng Jinshan Drawing Circles

Jinshan guided us
to the large stele at his family grave.

The stone, erected a few years ago,
was engraved with the names of
the latest five generations in Cheng family.

We asked Jinshan
to circle all the names of the AIDS victims.

It's easy.
Jinshan said.
Those at the top are too old and those at the bottom too young.
Ten years ago, no one sold blood.

Keeping mumbling,
he drew circles around the names in the middle
with a piece of chalk.

Cheng Guofu, Cheng Junfu, Cheng Junkui,
Cheng Chunshan, Cheng Tieliang, Cheng Tiecheng,
Cheng Tieshan, Cheng Jinshan...

He read out his own name.
One hand against the stone,
he used the other hand
to draw a white circle, clumsily, around it.

He didn't stop.
He kept drawing.

Tomb-Sweeping Day was yet to come.
Wheat sprouts were still green.
Clusters of new tombs
surrounded their ancestors.

They Were Houhan People

They were AIDS victims.
They were pathetic.
They were from Houhan Hamlet, Wenlou Village.
They were docile
and had been so for hundreds of years.
Even they themselves had said,
We are obedient.
They were the farthest away from the village council.
They were the most pathetic.
They were the wronged.
Why should they build roads for all the other hamlets
and not for us?
They were sad and indignant.
They had accumulated anger for hundreds of years.
They wanted to make some trouble.
Last month a woman in Wang Hamlet died
on her way to hospital.
They made a bit of trouble,
then they were rewarded with a road.
They learned this from others.
They looked aggressive.
They borrowed trucks and tractors.
They took collective actions.
They claimed they were on the edge of death, afraid of nothing.
They presented a petition to the county government.
They were beaten back.
They were in low spirits.
They became silent after coming back
except for a few old women

who covered their bleeding heads,
crying in the hamlet.
They were the ones who had suffered the hardest blows.
Their fellows told them to stand in front.
They said it was effective to have the weakest stand in front.
The old women were obedient.
The old women were hit by police batons.
The others ran away.
The others fled like wind.
They were clever.
They didn't get beaten.
They were Houhan people.
They were Henan people.

Cheng Junkui Died

When I returned from Europe,
Wu Ang told me on MSN,
Cheng Junkui died.

Cheng Junkui
who once worked as a sailor in Singapore,
who, in the photo,
had chubby cheeks,
was holding up a shark.

How is his wife?
As I blurted out
the question,
my face flushed a bit.

I met her just before Tomb-Sweeping Day.
A beautiful woman rarely seen in the village,
whose eldest daughter is now fifteen,
still looked a little shy with strangers.

She then wore a red ski coat.
When the nurse taught her to dance the waltz,
she slightly swung a leg in the sunlight
like a happy newlywed young woman.

I even thought
I might have fallen in love with her
if I hadn't known she was a victim.

Wu Ang said,
Don't mention her.
She has become 10 years older,
10 jin *thinner.*

RON WINKLER

Translated by Jake Schneider

For years, Ron Winkler's poems have been reporting back 'from the field'. Like him, his speakers are well-travelled, young David Attenborough types. Unlike many contemporary poets, they're still deeply invested in the natural world. But what they say about it – and the human structures that are never far off – is usually more revealing about ourselves as idiosyncratic, unreliable witnesses who try but often fail to unplug and soak in the moment.

Postcards and, by extension, postcard poems are incapable of telling it like it is. They're always written in a rush of tangents by distracted vacationers, and their envious recipients can't reconstruct the experiences that have been flattened onto the cardstock. Winkler embraces the limits of this format and adds in his own delightful poetic idiosyncrasies: invented words, grammar games, non-sequiturs.

Postcards from Territories, released in German this year, is as offhand and unexpected as all of Winkler's work, full of superbly scrambled language, but it takes this skewed view to the next logical step. This time the tangent is the subject. Reading them is like listening to someone retelling a dream and trying to visualize the out-of-reach images. The pictures of these postcards are in your mind.

Ron Winkler, *Karten aus Gebieten* © Schöffling & Co. Verlagsbuchhandlung GmbH, Frankfurt am Main 2017.

Postcards from Territories

26

We cruised upriver to the sea.
Only to defend ourselves.
The fakir district, a registered ski resort, was unlit
even by day.
A sizeable number are high up in the tanning chain. Their smocks
wear the KOHLHAAS logo.
Chances are they're checking whether the chemistry's still right.
They're pleasant folks, they love
unfiltered gasoline, and their tasers are quite user-friendly. Since yesterday
we've been staying
in one of those blood-coloured structures in the sub-suburbs,
drinking champagne
as a thrombosis prophylaxis. I went and got my trainer's licence
for fish. At nightfall, mosquito-sized phantoms
crawl out of the parkwork. They don't do much,
but they're alive.
When we dream back-to-back sleeps, they light up
with time.

25

By morning somebody had already activated
beauty. An ungrouped few opened up the bus and asked
me for relatives. Their motion quotient was off the charts.
But shortly thereafter they went unto the Lord.
That fell under dividends. What should I
say? Nature satisfies, has satisfied. Candles burn. The air extends
the cattle. And now businessman
is our pastime too. And we've got white crows
against the snow. Night falls while it's already there.
You sense a warm moon that gradually wanes you off
and, way out on the surfer, you see the sea beginning.

22

The medium is embarrassed. The mosquitoes regard
me as pleasant. In the morning of today gone by,
I danced in the boundless poppy blossom. Went blond.
I nearly wasn't catchable. Nor were the mosquitoes.
The builders have their own stethoscopes, for even the proximity
effect is spooky. Did their paths cross us? I can't be sure,
but while today's snow landed only in a 3.14 metre radius, it fell
straight across the city. Which perhaps is just a commercial district
with ample residential space. I'm better off for it; my resting heart rate
is a-b-b-a. And all under the misconstrued sun, no less.

8

Looking down from the acacia
is a most shiny sea. But the animals
have no tails. By night
they are marvellously mutable
and mighty. Touch seems
to be a dreamt-up river
reaching deep inland.
Some track the floral flotsam
downstream past miles upon miles
of apartment houses –
a scummy streak at shoulder level.
Once bought, flowers immediately
feed through a confetti machine.
And there is this nagging feeling
of being observed
through the turban eyes
of a much-too-large insect. And in them
being cold as the flesh
of the leviathan night.

31

I couldn't hold the contrail ray. Now we all drink
straight from the oracle, O pensatorial existence!
Matter-of-actual insects scurry us around. The wasps only sting
themselves. But that doesn't hustle them. The birds do well on
Mendelssohn, provided the moon hangs Islamic. Then it's high tide
under my eyelids in greenish-black minor. The secondborns wade
in kolk pools and wonder what next. They are fed
by cold lymph although the sun is burning. Incompatible with
my cultural, nor my stipulations. Still I sleep well,
and nuder by the night and more unsubstantiated. Spatballs in hand,
we claim we can intuit the eelpout's heartbeat.
That poutbeat, well preserved, makes the fairies
the largest. It could hardly be better: subtropical evenings, fruitings,
longings. That said: I did miss out on the quintessential sea.

30

Each day the container ship was a whole different
country. We stood on the quay, formed a Yes
in the sun's range of vision and watched what would happen. It transpired.
High tide, such fluke of nature, delivered a little white.
The Stradivariuses were worse at burning than we'd thought.
The seals didn't contribute the right surroundings.
It appeared easy but must have taken talent.
There was a steady buzzing. We drank map water and reentered
the ego anyway. Teenagers hitched rides through the parking structure
near the landing bridges. In demolished German.
As they please. Wish. I hope I never go to the same hospital
as my cohorts.

6

We hadn't made any plans to touch each other
but it happened.
A gleam without light.
And blackbirds.
As soon as we got there, we boarded
the remarkable.
Also, we had our lifelines
re-lasered.
The tone of voice
people use when talking to us is different now.
No longer the one for children.
The sea is like a mountain levelled by sunlight.
Where you can also swim to: geysers.
And blackbirds.
We feel totally
transformed by outlines.
What also stood out right away:
the TVs shedding
suspicious tears.
And blackbirds, parcelled out like a swarm
of bees.

YOHANNA JARAMILLO

Translated by Katrina Naomi

I came across Yohanna Jaramillo's poetry online, after a recommendation from the poet and translator David Shook. I was struck by Yohanna's writing from the off. I wrote to her to ask if I might translate a couple of her poems and began work on the two that appear here. My Spanish is pretty fluent but I'd only ever translated political texts before. There was a real sense of discovery in working on Yohanna's poems. I got a 'meaning' from the poems quite quickly but soon realised that there were things I hadn't quite caught and knew little about. I researched Mexican political issues but some of the more scientific language had me stumped – even in English. I went back to Yohanna, always working in Spanish, she helped to fill in my rather poor knowledge of all things scientific, then I redrafted the poems. After putting the new drafts aside for a while, I read them aloud, reworked them several more times, then sent them to Yohanna explaining what I thought the poems were saying and asking for any corrections. She asked a friend to read the poems too and came back with some suggestions. We batted ideas backwards and forwards, I edited the poems again, then sent her final versions.

I've really enjoyed doing these translations, these are the first that I've done, and I'd love to do more. I'd welcome suggestions of other poets I might work with. The rhythms of Yohanna's poetry have stayed with me. I very much hope other people will enjoy reading her work, she deserves a far wider audience.

Open Letter

If you knew you went inside me after ten at night,
and were the reason for the spliff at 4.20 in the morning,
and something extra, like the expected email,
the call
      which is always answered.
If you knew that each verse I write
I re-read, in delay mode, for you;
I know how to manage brainwaves,
I know about metals and energy,
I know about carbon and my antenna-hair,
I know that fire and vegetables gather,
I know the secret of broccoli:
It wants to be the drag queen of vegetables.
I know that the only thing that doesn't grow with heat and water
is time,
that's why the sun is ecstatic,
that's why this planet is worried.
I know that all the masses which float
belong to us, we belong to them, we belong to each other.
And we spin,
and our rushing spins,
you don't catch up and we spin,
I write the truth and we spin.

The chemical elements of our bones,
the quarks, make us rotate
and we spin,
without vomiting, we spin,
a slow-motion turn,

the spinning top of 'someone' who explodes with the launch's speed,
at top speed, the particles fall apart,
and they said 'another turn and we go', and they went and left us, spinning.
If you knew, I say, like the @ncient poet,
as if modern verbs didn't exist
when we speak of love,
of this rare creation of society,
which is addictive.
That's why I write this with a dropper,
I'm a slow learner,
I'm accused of lacking ethics,
in this investigation.

This Isn't a Yellow Cake

These aren't the six thousand or three point two million years
in the radiocarbon calibration curve,
it's not as if they were Neanderthals or Africans,
it's not as if a third race or a fourth has been created
from the same Universe
and definitely from the same substance.
It matters if we ate each other,
if some of us bled,
if we were naked,
if buildings fell on us.
I embrace all decisions,
all those historical facts,
even Feynman.
We all went down,

we all went down in a literal sense,
maybe we will all float
on a surfboard,
on the earth's crust.
Between the void
and the void is not a natural number
created to find the route to the matrix (S).
As the young Leyva said: *all realities exist.*

I accept all beliefs,
Lucy and my ancestors' imaginary friends, such as Eve,
are welcome.
Atapuerca and all the tunnels under the sea
are welcome.
The soldiers who return to see their children,
and their adopted pets,
are welcome.
The Panama Canal, Disney, part of Chiapas and all the recreations
    of the world,
are welcome.
But Oxxo and McDonald's
are not welcome.
Medicines, toothpastes, deodorants
are not welcome.
Coca Cola, ICE that can't be swallowed, heads of state
are not welcome.
Discoveries made by a fragile mind
do us little good.
O children of Coltán!
O children of Chernobyl!
O children of Rome!

O children of the lower case!
When they play hide and seek with 'God',
he gets lost.
Before they find him, he drops Uranium gas
and destroys them.

NOTE: Richard Philips Feynman, (1918–1988) was a US physicist and Arturo Beltrán Leyva was the former head of a Mexican drug cartel.

JÁNOS PILINSZKY

Translated by Clive Wilmer and George Gömöri

János Pilinszky (1921–81) is probably the greatest Hungarian poet of the post-war period. He is best remembered for his poems of the 1950s which bear witness to the horrors of the Second World War and mid-twentieth-century Europe. Three selections have appeared in English: *Selected Poems* translated by Ted Hughes and János Csokits (Carcanet, 1976; later expanded as *The Desert of Love* (Anvil, 1989)), *Crater* by Peter Jay (Anvil, 1978) and *Passio: Fourteen Poems* (Worple, 2012) by Clive Wilmer and George Gömöri. These volumes overwhelmingly emphasise the work of the 1950s. The two poems published here, both from the 1970s, typify his later poetry – austerely economical and enigmatic, with the outlook of a Christian Existentialist, who feels abandoned by God. The first of this pair addresses the most admired of all modern Hungarian poets, Attila József (1905–37), whose tragic and socially alert poetry arose from a working-class childhood of extreme poverty.

Attila József Again

You: foot soldier of the universe.
Me: of somewhere else, a cadet.
I would sacrifice my officer's gloves
for the sake of your soldier's kit.

Rembrandt

The father's house: ashes and vinegar.
A kiss and a hand-kiss: ashes and vinegar.
Closed eyes in the grave and in the bed,
a discipline persisting after death.

CRÌSDEAN MACILLEBHÀIN
(CHRISTOPHER WHYTE)

Translated by Niall O'Gallagher

The three poems translated here were written in Budapest in the spring of 2004. They develop Crìsdean MacIlleBhàin's practice of using a suppressed language, Gaelic, to approach repressed or unspeakable subjects. In the first, which addresses the Italian sculptor Agostino di Duccio's *Angel of the Annunciation*, the speaker waits for a silence to be broken. *Vers libres*, which had been the dominant mode of Scottish Gaelic poetry since the 1970s, becomes the exception in MacIlleBhàin's work. In 'Portrait of a Father', the poem's unwillingness to settle upon a regular metre reflects the speaker's inability to come up with a concept of loving fatherhood to replace the figure of his actual father. By contrast, the thirteen couplets of the final poem observe a pitiless syllabic regularity which seems to ground the extreme nature of the situation described as the speaker imagines his father's corpse rotting inside its coffin. Whichever form they deploy, MacIlleBhàin's poems continue to stretch his language, putting old words to new uses. This public poetry is paradoxically discreet as it exploits both the frankness of the Gaelic tradition and the intimacy its modern poetry assumes with those who can approach it directly. The challenge for a translator into English is to find a voice that allows the word to resound not as a shout, as he says elsewhere, but as a whisper, 'since whispering will do'.

Angel, You Bow Your Head...

Angel, you bow your head
in a still half-graceful movement,
every colour you had is gone
but the burnished dun of
the hard-wrought clay from when
you were first made. Won't you

deliver your message from
that faded square of paper on
the wall beside the window that
looks out on what's left of the snow
on the roofs of the nearby houses?
I'd love to find relief

from this unmoving anguish
but you won't open your lips
your lily has no scent
and I can only wait in hope
for the far-off day when you awake
and my hearing notices your speech.

Portrait of a Father

That's it, I have the canvas now,
it's ready, I could put
wood around it, even a gilded frame,
decorated with flowers and little fruits,
as if someone important were
set to appear in the middle,
and I stop... what am I going to do
now? What can I do with this emptiness?
How can I fill in this white space?

If I don't hurry, who's to say
you won't appear there yourself,
the father who, for me, was nothing
more than an emptiness, perfectly white,
that wounded my eyes with its glare
until I understood why it was there,
because of everything it had to hide.

Maybe that blindness
is to blame for all those years I spent
as a dreamer, ransacking
every tradition, each folk-tale
until I knew every way a child could be
conceived without a father,
every story people had dreamt up.

I will not count them here,
because, despite that multiplicity,
the kaleidoscope of colour I found,

it still might be beyond me
to keep you from appearing in the canvas
that could be so lovely, so free
if I could keep it unsullied.

I've done a different kind of ransacking –
I'm always doing it, even today,
on buses and trains.
on every pavement my foot falls upon –
I keep making notes
about every pair I see,
each father with his son, each son and father
especially when the son
is just an infant.

How does he talk to him?
What sort of gestures does he make,
the set of his lips, the look in his eyes
when he helps his little son
with his coat, or when he sets him up
as well as he can
on a chair that's far too high?
What is it that he feels?
It was so simple,
the question oppressing me,
that gave me no rest:
What is fatherhood?

Who's to say I couldn't
fill in the canvas,
give life to the emptiness

with everything I saw at those times,
though that absence would be like a book
in which I'd write words
in an unknown tongue,
putting them together bit by bit
in sentences, perhaps,
whose purport I wouldn't grasp.

Were the glare to lessen,
should the white grow paler,
I'd see traces of wickedness
and of madness too,
the madness that was a way
to rein in the memory of wickedness.
And a different tale would appear
imagined by one
who refused to believe what reached his ears
of the wickedness of fathers, families:
the story of a son who slayed his father
and won a place at his mother's side
in the bed where he was once conceived.

I'm overcome with tiredness!
I'm not a painter,
though I would love to wrap the knowledge of
fatherhood around me like a cloak,
or to walk the city's pavements with
the thought I had – of a father who'd remember
each day when he awoke he had a son,
though he was an old man, and his son
a father too. The thought of his son

would be as close to him as his own skin,
as the state of his skin, it would not leave him
but when he was asleep and even then
his son would appear to him
in his dreams, painted,
as they say, with the colours of love.
That thought would be as wound up
in his everyday affairs
as the scent of his own skin.

But you were my father, only you,
you yourself, you cannot be changed.
So, I'll strike the untouched canvas
deliberately, so that the lines of your face
will no longer appear there,
nor your threatening glance, but the world.

You'll Reach the Grave's Edge Without Admitting...

You'll reach the grave's edge without admitting,
it will be buried with you; the word

that could have allowed us to reconcile
will never now be heard among the living.

I got no news of the lips of the dead,
do they move restlessly beneath the sods,

still trembling until the maggots have
devoured them all, until, mercilessly,

the teeth and all the bones that ever could
have formed a word when you still had the chance

are exposed. I don't know if the damp
of the elements that soak down through

the earth, seeping through the coffin lid,
reaches an unmoving cheek, trickles down

as if it were a tear, or the right number
of days and months that have to pass before

there's so little difference between
what once was firm and what was liquid

in your eyes, or the area around them,
that you even forget what weeping was.

Won't one act of goodness or heroism
remain, that can be taken from your grave

and not this enduring cowardice!
Instead, I'll bear it carefully away,

the word you never uttered, and I'll set
it resounding, in my poems, in my life.

BAKHYT KENJEEV

Translated by J. Kates

Bakhyt Kenjeev is an elusive guy. He slips around the world like quicksilver, from Montréal to Central Asia, and yet remains, like quicksilver, elemental, always himself, a Russian poet, you have to say a post-Soviet poet, imbued as his poems are in the culture that bred him (although a statement like this is embarrassingly and deceptively reductive). Even as he cruises Lake Champlain at the turn of the new millennium, 'the crush at the cashier | is old stuff to a Moscow student'. And the lake is not his only waterway. Always in flux, a divine river of time never flows far from even the lightest of his lines. Kenjeev is not a poet I read in order to translate, but one I translate in order to read, using the discipline to align my own attention with his. While remaining conscious of the poet's form, I have always been far more concerned with his tone. In this, Kenjeev has encouraged me. 'The absence of rhyme doesn't bother me at all,' he has reassured me more than once. And yet, it continues to bother me, because form is part of this poet's playfulness.

Here is a Proud Man with a Contented Grimace...

Here is a proud man with a contented grimace
who drinks strong wine and eats mutton.
He knows by heart all human speech,
he lords it over his woman every evening,
while his woman, laughing, cooks his supper,
and afterwards, she lords it over her husband.

But temptation comes to afflict this fellow,
working to turn him into a spiritual cripple.
Back from a funeral, he stares silently at the wall,

with a lupine smile he exudes that black humour
the ancient Greeks called melancholy
and there is no more happiness in his person.

Overcoming his weakness and indolence,
he goes out into the kitchen and falls to his knees –
hands joined, humility in his countenance,
and a thirst to know the truth by serious conversation
with that one who sits in heaven on a throne
and dispassionately regulates human existence.

He fails to remember that there is no dialogue
with anyone on a throne, it's always one-sided,
this weary slave in the gloom of the Russian night
raises a single problem in his anxious prayer:
'Tell me, o God of lovingkindness, that there is no death!'
But he hears in response, '... and no eternal life either...'

Where Heavy Bread is Humid and Porous...

Where heavy bread is humid and porous,
and the surface of a swelling grape
is dull, like an unpolished green-eyed
agate, where nothing is to be expected

from running water and enduring stone, where a ray
(a sprout of light) lightly like a child
erupts on earth – not furiously, not a thorn
or a sunset in a crevice of life? No, gentle.

I love you. And words, not spoken enough
in the dark, remain alive,
as in melancholy twilight, on the hills
a roll-call of apple-tree and olive.

Lake Champlain

I'm footloose – the hoariest of freedoms.
The cliffs are agate, a bundle of firewood
A bassoon, the overgrown path a cat's paw.
The ferry is crowded, but the crush at the cashier
is old stuff to a Moscow student –
slipped in sideways I'm already on the gangway.

The steps I take creak ominously
as in a childhood dream. I'm perfectly
unafraid. Underworld, terrestrial,
overhead... And I'm laughing, breathing
on the sheltered side. One traveller
is smoking weed, while the others –

one holds a Bible, one fiddles silently
with a cheap amulet, in mourning for
the eloquent light. Look, my
comrade, death knows no shame,
and the little houses of Vermont forever
reflected in water that will not return.

CELESTIAL BRIZUELA

Translated by Laura Chalar

The self-assurance in Argentinian poet Celestial Brizuela's poems is deceptive: with their current of darkness underlying the daylight and flowers, with their hints at suppressed violence, they are more difficult than their airy format would imply. Celestial's interest in visual imagery connects her two callings (poetry and filmmaking) and is very evident in the lush poems showcased here, which I enjoyed translating, as I think they travel well from one language to the other.

Magnolias

◆

In the breathing
a man saw me shaking among magnolias.

I gathered earth with my hands while
he arranged the conchs in my hair.

He thought I was the Queen of the Sea
(I)
(who can barely float)

The Cap

I go to the meeting that pierces the closet's scream.
To me, the blood in the glass jar,
that does not concern me.

I dismissed the creatures from your house,
it scared you to see me so much my own.
You wanted from my body
preservation
and every night you fanatically went
to make sure that the jar cap
was screwed on tight.

I woke up claustrophobic.

Then you would tell me:

'It's for love that I do it,
so that it won't evaporate.'

If I Tell Him...

◆

A contraction in his cheekbone if I tell him no.
In the inner courtyards of buildings
laundry seems
to come undone
from the clothesline.

◆

God liked to see me soak my pillow in sweat.
I made no wishes.
I wanted him to see me opening like a butterfly
(inhabiting desire)
as wide open as possible –
I felt a thousand animals inside me.
'Cover me in fingerprints,' I said to him,
but he was asleep.

Spring

◆

The sun-rooted mouth
opened
a flowering of carnations.

It appeared, darkling,
inside an orchard, air
no longer coming out.

On the other side
windows were yellow.

VASALIS

Translated by David McKay

Vasalis published these six poems during her lifetime, between 1940 and 1954. For the rest of her long life, she declined to share her poetry with the public.

'Fear' and 'Death', two of her earliest published poems, illustrate her piercing intelligence and fascination with inner life. Her liberated approach to poetic form is also on display here; the lines expand and contract as needed, and her malleable rhyme schemes create subtle musical patterns that support rather than distracting from her vivid, plainspoken voice. 'Death' shows a sardonic wit reminiscent of Dorothy Parker, yet the poem closes with a mysterious, hopeful moment of elusive insight – a shift characteristic of Vasalis's work.

'Phoenix I', 'Phoenix II' and 'Child' form a series inspired in large part by the loss of her young son Dicky to polio during the German occupation of the Netherlands. These visionary poems move from dream to the waking world to memory, testifying to the intricacy of human emotion and the artistic imperative to wrest beauty from suffering. 'Child' recalls the catharsis of Greek tragedy. The classical spirit and the elegiac theme of premature death also echo through her later poem 'To a Tree in Vondelpark'.

Vasalis left behind many other poems when she died in 1998, some of which were, at her request, published by her children in 2002. A selection of these posthumous poems, also translated by David McKay, appeared in the online magazine *The High Window* in 2017.

Fear

I've been afraid of almost everything:
of darkened rooms, of figures in the carpet,
of silence, of the hollering
of hawkers in the evening, of a party,
of glances on the tram, and of myself.
Those are the old familiar kinds of fear.
But now there's one thing that I fear above all else;
it could destroy me, so I bury it
under a flood of facts, till it comes back again:
the moment when I see my landlady appear,
entering my bedroom in the bitter light of morning,
the blunt look on her face an obvious warning
of what she'll say: no letter yet, my dear.

Death

Death pointed out some small but fascinating things:
here is a nail – Death said – and here is rope.
I look at him, a child. He is my master.
for he's the one I trust, my only hope,
my Death.

He showed me everything: the pills, the drinks to cook,
the pistols, gas taps, where the roof is steep,
a bath, a razor blade, a snow-white sheet
'in case' one day I should decide to look
for death.

Before he left, he gave me something, too:
a locket with a portrait. 'Does this ring a bell?
Well, who knows, maybe someday it could help,
if you decide you won't be going through
with dying,
but who's stopping you?'
said Death.

Phoenix I

I had a dream in wartime that the war had come.
A wooden aircraft dropped out of the skies
and ploughed a teetering track through the tall grass
until it stopped with moaning, song, and sighs.

As if from a sick ark the injured animals came,
one of each kind, and straggled to a tent
that I was decorating like the heavens
with grass, trees, and a starry firmament.

Then suddenly I saw, on a long white
table, an ash-grey bird. Its head bore a blue mark
like a blue fire, burning with upright heat
out on a distant hilltop in the dark.

Was the bird injured? Did it need my care?
Around my finger I felt its small, dry talons close
and there we stood as midnight paled to dawn,
motionless morning, and a new sun rose.

And when I looked down at my hand I saw
the finger it was clasping had turned blue
and wrote a line of verse, the bird still blazing…
Then it looked back, as if to grant its blessing.

Phoenix II

Tonight, during a quiet visit to a friend –
our words like swarms of bees that glittered over a field –
it shot out like a bird from the dense grass
where it had lain protected and concealed:

a yearning rush straight for the sky
and with a cry I thought that everyone could hear.
Then I discovered who was flying out of me
and who had chosen my flame as his high lair.

O little phoenix, my too-brief possessor –
I see the deep blue bonfires of his eyes,
the slight weight on my hand, on which he sat;
I hear his singing wings, and then he flies...

Don't hurry, do not shriek with pain, o hand.
Write on until your fingers all have burned.

Child

There was a slight warmth lingering over his face:
the earth at night, after the sun has gone.
Like wind that moves through curtains, a slight breath
entered his lips and wandered out again...

For he was life, exposed almost without a shell,
and nothing but life, poured till overfull,
and tumbling down without a stain or shadow
and rising till it brimmed the fragile bowl.

How broad the passageway to life still seemed
and how wide open to his ebb and flow...
How slight and still and beautiful his death
left him out on the empty beach alone.

To a Tree in Vondelpark

A tree was felled, a tree with long green locks.
It sighed and rustled like a child
even as it fell, still full of summer wind.
I saw the cart they used to drag it off.

Oh, like a young man, like tall Hector lashed to Achilles' car,
with streaming hair and with the smell of youth
flowing from his fair wounds,
his head, still perfect, on the ground,
his noble torso still unmarred.

A BLOSSOM SHROUD

Focus on the Poets of Shubbak

GOLAN HAJI

Translated by Stephen Watts and the author

Golan Haji is a Kurdish Syrian poet who writes in Arabic and presently lives in Paris. We met in Syria at the al-Mallajeh Festival in August 2010 and began translating each other's work. Subsequently we've been able to meet in London and Paris and have continued our translating. This present gathering of poems was commissioned by Shubbak (the one exception being 'The Feather and The Mirror' which was written earlier) in time for the July 2017 Festival.

Many of the poems hark back to early memories, from the poet's Kurdish childhood, but also to his readings and experiences as a young man in the 1990s (for instance in the poem 'The End Of Days'). In fact strong elements of Kurdish mythology, imagery, folklore and village life run right through the poems, especially in the presence of the snake, which in his grandmother's remembered words, is as much guardian, mentor and friend, as enemy or threat; and which, with the ouroboros, makes of beginning and end a simultaneity or continuity. Painful recent histories are thus being read in the light of memories that preceded them, and his Arabic is being written through a Kurdish lens.

Mystic Islamic references also abound, particularly to al-Tabari's *History Of Nations and Kings*, and also to the saying that in the belly of every snake is an image of the devil. The snake image is seen through an awareness of the Ragnarok of Norse mythology, and of Ezequiel Martínez Estrada's 'Ouroboros' and Osamu Dazai's *The Setting Sun* as well. The preoccupation with something painfully ended, but acting as a starting point, as a point of change, a strong cycle-circle of new beginnings runs through the poems and through life beyond them. Other markers include paintings seen in Paris and elsewhere: works by Pierre Bonnard and Anselm Kiefer among them. Thus the poet believes the visual power of words matters as much as their music and logic. Dream and invention are at the heart of the poems – as the poet said to

me: 'When I remember I dream and invent at the same time.' The Arabic
of these poems is infused with the poet's Kurdish memory: we have tried
to bring these aspects and qualities over into the English translation.

The End Of Days

after Anselm Kiefer
for Elena Lydia Scipioni

A snake with honey-coloured eyes survived and told what had happened:

In our burning fields, Yesterday drew me with the spittle of its mouth on a
charred wall, like a blackboard in front of frightened pupils. Thus you saw
in me the image of my father, throwing my last pennies into the fountain
of death, then sewing the buttons of his oil-green coat in the furrows of
mud where you had planted seeds, arranged in the form of words, and
they grew and blossomed when light rained down warm as remorse, and
again blood was made to flow on the palms of the earth. Canes grew high
as poplars and we broke them to roof our refuge, and we jumped over our
vein-streams to swim in our first sky. We fertilised our language with our
debris. Mountains had become ripe heads for the fists of the sky and the
slopes cheeks we ran down like melted ice, and at every point where the
disappeared had fallen an unattainable flower sprang up, or a burning
matchstick flickered before a schoolboy could close his mouth over it to
put out the flame – as he hurries to do his homework on forgetting fear.

We will remember for a long time how we were before this harvest. Each of
us will visit his own grave, carrying a whip on his shoulder, or behind his
back a sickle or a knife. Time was a game. We bade farewell to our beds

that had been smashed by our dreams. Gamblers offered us a moon that crumbled to dust at the touch of our fingers. Rats offered us their eyes as stars. Hunger blazed its suns behind our foreheads. Books we hadn't read flittered down and landed on our ulcers. Great silences seeped through our bandages. No one uttered a word. The dots and signs with which we ended our lines leapt towards the words scattered about them, and all meanings changed.

The Old Christ

after Pierre Bonnard
for Jinane Abbadi

1

There's no cure for this hesitancy.
An unease you're familiar with,
        like a river rippling between two enemies
                quietly ebbing back.
Who shot you?
The flashbulb befuddled you into losing your balance
        and you duped your fear by smelling a rose
                no one sees in the dust but you,
you the emaciated, who fasted for forty days.
Detesting the touch of water and miracles,
        you created a wedding fish from white wine,
                bathing women from the dust of peaches.
Fascinated by imperfection, you missed the final touch.

2

Who fought you?
Are your fists a little clenched
		because there are camera lenses in every corner,
				and the perplexed and miserable have nowhere to hide?
This evening, God sparks April's lightning,
		photographing what's unseen in the womb.
The dead are blowing a forgotten organ tune in the birch trunks,
and you are standing alone, eyes lowered and chest naked,
		your reddened face a bolted door hammered by hands,
				blistered by the sun and the shame.
		Your tongue abstains from any blow,
you standing alone, a boxer no longer holding brush or gloves
		in an arena he never leaves
		because he is unable to depart,
				not knowing where he can go.

'Were It Not For The Three Pleasures Afforded To Youth...'

The idea that Salvation is catalysed by malady.

No mirror to view my face or nullify my pallor or the asphyxiation of my features. I'll stop worrying. Let me be visited by a punishment I don't deserve. Trembling and helpless, I surrender to the fever.

And I become a little calmed and I say to myself:

Deceive life and live as a convalescent, an insomniac, a drunkard:

You, young man I don't know, measure with your lips the temperature of my forehead, before the eye wilts and the glance is broken, before the throat dries up and sweat oozes with scandalous sourness. Craving a heart that cannot be heard, a lucidity that comes after secret grieving, a calm you've never tasted – be someone in a fever who is healed by himself, not a hostage who silently anticipates his execution because the most terrible thing had already happened and he has come to terms with the sentence of death. Be a drunkard whose knees and teeth are shaking from the cold of March. Be someone who sleeps a little then is knocked over by a blade of grass.

NOTE: the title is a half line from the 'Mu'allaqa' (Suspended Ode) of Tarafa Ibn al-'Abd

A New Life?

A month of cloud came to an end this morning
            with a ray of sun entering my empty post-box
                    with its dust particles, I glimpsed it
                            as I went out.
Coming back from the night,
            with messages of grass from the prisoners' cemetery,
            with wet eyes, I talked to myself like a madman,
I switched off my lamp and prepared myself

to begin in silence my day that was splintered by the years
and to step aside slowly on the iron bridge,
amid those running to catch their trains,
a guilty man whose only defence is light.

The Feather And The Mirror

(A Fairytale from 'God's Cinema')

When the Kurd met the she-djinn he was blinded by light and
fainted. She put a little mirror under his nose and its silver surface
became clouded, then she put a feather there and its down trembled.
She felt relieved knowing that he was asleep and that the groanings
she heard were not those of death but of his long dreamings: 'I love
him and he'll stay alive' she said.

The only condition the king of the djinns put on his approval of the
marriage of the Kurd and the she-djinn was he should never show
anger to her face. The wedding went on in the wilderness for many
days and nights, djinns ignited their eyes like torches out in the
mountains that the guests would arrive at the place of dancing and
fires walked in the air among the dancers without burning anyone,
and jugs of juice were circulated from mouth to mouth. In order not
to make the djinns afraid of the ruses of the Kurdish relatives,
blacksmiths melted silver pins brought from pillows and dresses and
birth gowns and with small hammers they fashioned necklaces and
wristlets to dowry the bride.

Days dragged by, months, years. The Kurd and the she-djinn begot
children whose skins were white as milk spilt over snow, with fingers

tender and pudgy like the cigarettes of mountain folk. And the best-beloved of the Kurd's heart was the stubbornest. One day this stubborn boy disappeared into the wilderness and didn't come back. By the middle of the following day the father returned exhausted from echoing shouts throughout the valleys and caves, and he was enraged by his wife's words: 'Don't worry, he'll stay alive and he'll come back.' And he forgot his promise and became angry at her. With every word of blame and reproach a part of her body disappeared and the angry man became blind seeing nothing. By the time he'd calmed down the wife was entirely gone, and what remained of the children were just half-bodies, but their shadows on the soil were whole. Their mother remained with them without anyone being able to see her.

While Leaving A Sunny Room A Voice Called Saying: 'Stay'

The spider's house
    in the right angle of the northern window
    has not been touched by the wind –
        a black house imprinted on your window like traces
            of a seal on the stamp of a letter
                returned unopened to the sender –
you noticed it when you cleansed your eyeglasses of fingerprints and
                                  the dust of days
    with a piece of your grandmother's headscarf,
        and pulled back a curtain of branches and leaves:
        your narrow road still is muddy.

You don't savour the cold.
Were it not for these days, you said,
    my life that's been confused by spring
        would be a cloud that rained only on me
        and changed the colours of that hill:
            from pistachio-green fluttering above my grandfather's grave
            to the sky-blue of my daughter's eyes.

A Tree Whose Name I Don't Know

No bell rings and no one comes.
How many days have passed
    without message or phone call
        where I locked myself in and lost the key.
            And I too sent no message and phoned no one.
I who am tormented, bandaged and wilted by words
I talk to you, tree whose name I don't know:
    neither my hunger nor my thirst matter
        since I've sucked on the tenderness of your silence.

Alone I've come to you, to sit beneath your vast mercy;
I am small: a blossom begets me in white oblivion,
        a blossom shrouds me, the breeze follows my funeral;
I don't caress girls nor do they caress me,
and like you I don't know my name.
Poor are my words –
    that rise and fall like the hiccups of a babe-in-arms –
        in the haze of another language,

and my skin talks to you:
with a thousand small mouths it drinks sunlight with you –
        the sun of my ancestors whose hair turned white
                in their childhoods when they panicked,
                        terrified by the revenge of wounded serpents;
nobody knew how long the horror would last
        or until when the serpents would keep swimming in the waters
                                                of dream
until the harsh became tender and the hair at their temples
                whitened.

My grandfather aged in his youth;
paralysed by a stray bullet, treatable only by pain:
        they laid him down on a rug of goat's hair,
                motionless and naked,
        they locked the door and windows to his clay chamber
                and released the wasps;
in his house, white beneath the April sun,
        he waited for quickening pace to return to his feet.

Like him, like you, my waiting has been for too long –
dead hours are my most fertile:
are they happy, the old people of this country I came to
                as a guest?
Happiness here is as white as old age;
I see the fearful – infuriated and shouting –
        and behind my dark eyes
                two gods are slaying a sleeping prisoner.
O tree whose name I don't know:
        each trembling blossom is hope arrived,
                your petals have fallen on the crown of my white hair,

and for this long waiting my roots have turned white
　　　　like my mother's hair in the dark years;
silently I talk to you –
　　　　I whose fear has become sadness
　　　　and you whom beauty startled into blossom.

Crescent

You thinned your pain.

As a boy, on the frontier, you placed it like a small coin under the wheels
　　　　　　　　　　　　　　　　　　　of a train
and a girl you loved made herself a necklace of it in the fields

Smugglers taught you how to strike it in the quiet
　　　　in the night with the hammers of thieves
　　　　　　　　to conceal your finger marks in front of others

You thinned it with silence, with long walks
until it became transparent and hard
　　　　like a cut nail disappeared in the carpet of time

And when you found it
it had become a moon eaten away by love
　　　　and you hung it in the sky of your soul

And stayed awake all alone, waiting for the *azhan* of Eid.

The Mud Milk Bar

for Jano and Nuh

After two long days of fear in the streets of our city, this morning, on the
phone, my sister let me hear sparrows quarrelling over dry bread in the
little courtyard of the house they'd moved to several years ago.

An owl soared inside my head, an owl the moon had silvered and sent to us,
descending from the hilltop – where the Yezidis bury each other –
    to the beds installed in front of the houses and on the kitchen roofs,
    fenced in by curtains white as the screens
where the moon projects its silent films in blue and silver,
thin-walled boxes with lids removed which sleep has opened
                    to the universe;

With the headlamps of his van the driver woke the old man who had been
sleeping, ill under the stars of September, so he rose up to receive us,
lame, his femur fixed with screws, superstitiously cursing the one who'd
invented the name 'Death's Fracture', and he slaughtered a rooster for our
banquet; his son brought us a home-made arak distilled three times from
black figs, a little of which we sprinkled onto plates of tomato and white
cheese with black cumin seed, in a tiny shop made of mud. 'Lion's milk is
heavy on empty bellies' he said and took us outside to sit on straw chairs,
where we carried on in silence under God's lamp and iced white arak
soothed our palms: a cool breeze brushed our bare arms, coming from
the cotton fields, irrigated and blossoming, there where the moon had
sent us an owl that swooped down, low and silently, nearby

The night was spread across wide expanses
Entrancing was the beating of wings,
Pure the chanting of insects.

We wandered drunk in the night of our innocence, in the night journey
of our return, across the earthen paths that led each of us to the house
that was his true home; one among us, who mocked poetry and cotton
festivals, who devoured lettuce in secret, fell to his knees, shouting and
rolling on the straw ash in his uncle's fields, weeping his lost love, our
shirts were muddied by his tears when we carried him, avoiding the last
gunshots of those returning from the last wedding of the season, hearing
laughter guffawing from loud speakers as guests burnt garlands of green
banknotes. As stealthily as possible we took narrow dark alleys until we
reached his home; we woke at daybreak, under the smiles of our sisters:
how could we tell the long hard pillows of our mothers from the white
watermelons on which we'd lain our heads, like dwarves who place their
heads on the fingers of a giant, or like small boys whose palms touch a
woman's thigh, while we had been collapsing with happiness, snoring
under rustling pine trees on the cold, smooth cement that was hennaed
with spots printed by chimneys that had rusted through the winters.

Truth sharpens its fangs on the bones of the forgotten.
Naked is my grown soul.
Owl, you mouth of time that has silvered my temples,
          and savaged the sparrows sleeping on the mulberry branches,
how did you catch the snake whose head my mother tried to trample
          barefoot in her childhood,
     when it escaped such human fear and lived its long life?
Is it because it closed its eyes like a woman preparing for love,
     and slowed its pace to shed its past?
     Quietly, it took off the leather dress,
          glimmering under God's lamp amid the blossoming cotton.

'It Rains from Heaven and Earth': Five Arabic and Kurdish poets

Introduced by Golan Haji

I was with a group of poets on a long journey across Tunisia in August 2011. The bus of poets was stopped by traffic police, because the driver exceeded the speed limit to reach the hotel before *iftar*. On the highway, in the stopped bus, I heard Ziad Abdelkader's voice on the phone and discovered some of his poems through the well-known poet Awlad Ahmad. In fact one of the policemen knew some of Awlad Ahmad's poems by heart.

Other coincidences that led me to read other poets are no less haphazard. However, the reason for gathering together these five poets is not only that this is one result of my mutual work in translation with Stephen Watts over the past months, but essentially because Arabic and Kurdish cultures have many things in common, and share the same geography, in the north of both Syria and Iraq, as do the Assyrian and the Syriac, where multilingualism has thrived for millennia.

Readers might have missed what emerges quietly from these blurred and tragic days in the Middle East. These poets are predisposed to the personal and the private, envisioning their own imaginary land which poetry can bring across languages against the confines of dominating tongues and societies when maps are being brutally redrawn worldwide. They are neither heroes nor are they rebellious. They write inwardly, though their poetry is not complacently solipsistic. Their poems stretch beyond their own traditions, and are characterized by a vigorous pluralism.

Nasr Jamil Shaath (b. 1979) left besieged Gaza in 2009 and settled in Norway where he worked with fishermen on the Atlantic shores. With an apparent preference for the role of a keen observer of daily life, he calmly addresses the unseen and overlooked ordinary, and interrogates the uncomfortable until it becomes familiar. Nasr lives now in Marrakech, and he wrote these poems after an accident, when he was hit by a car in the north of Norway.

Ziad Abdelkader (b. 1979) is the only poet here who still lives in his first country, Tunisia. He says he has multiple pasts. History in his poems is contemporary, and his desire is to present what can be done in poetry through subtle means, from his early lyric poetry dedicated to Saadi Youssef, Mahmoud Darwish and other Arab poets or reaching out to imaginary places when he invents poems and attributes them at times to Russian poets and film makers.

The other three poets are Syrian Kurds. They learnt to write in Kurdish without support and by themselves, since their mother tongue had been officially banned in Syria, where there was a risk of linguicide, as the nationalist regimes, as it were, had targeted Kurdish for extinction.

Ameer Alhussein (b. 1980) and Reber Youssef (b. 1981) write in both Kurdish and Arabic. Their poems here were translated from Arabic. Both were part of a group of young poets who published *inferno*, a magazine for new poetry, in 2009, in Kurdish and Arabic – but in book form because censorship in Syria didn't allow them to launch a literary journal.

Ameer Alhussein continues writing and translating for Arabic newspapers from Erbil, where he now lives, a Kurdish foreigner and refugee in Kurdistan of Iraq. Reber Youssef lives in Germany, and his cinematic allegiance to landscape allows him to transform his concerns visually into scenes of the past.

Ciwan Qado (1980) also lives in Germany and he writes only in Kurdish. We translated his poems from Kurmanji, the dialect of the Kurdish part of Syria. I had to scrutinize every poem, and consult the poet for almost every word. The strangest often sounds natural in poetry, so Stephen kept some literal translations, wherever possible in English, like 'it rains from heaven and earth' which is the Kurmanji equivalent of 'it rains cats and dogs'.

Uprooted poets have their roots in the air they breathe everywhere. Poets might pass their lives in a permanent diaspora among languages, and poetry might be, to put it in Stephen Watts's words, a 'journey across breath'. We translated these poems intermittently, first in Malmö in autumn 2016, and then in Paris where we finished the translations during rainy and snowy days, in Montmartre and Saint Denis, during late winter and early spring 2017.

NASR JAMIL SHAATH

Translated by Golan Haji and Stephen Watts

I Am A Handful Of Wheat, Life Grinds Me And I Eat Of It

To descend slowly
is the habit of the sad.
On the threshold they cast rapid glances over their shoulders.
He who is the constant plaything of sadness
himself plays as a child does
who counts the stairs

In My Life...

In my life
I've heard many marvellous words
that astonished me and made me weep
and led me back to this earth.
But I'm still longing for the early years
of language that loosened Adam's tongue
and let him soothe himself
like a stranger.

The Sea is Wider Than its Name in my Mouth...

The sea is wider than its name in my mouth
and my glance across it wider still.
So I spoke to myself
like a tourist just descended from a liner
who treats his estrangement by looking
one more time at a bird in the sky.

Hope is as White...

Hope is as white
as the lining of a black trouser pocket
plunge your hand deep inside and
out comes empty lining.

I Have Faults...

I have faults
in my life that are inadvertent,
like a mechanic who rubs his hands
with sand touched by neither bullet nor seed
after repairing a car that will
transport a family away from war...
then he washes his hands with water and white soap
that he places on a stone forgetting
to cleanse it of his hands' dirt.

Whenever I Picked up a Morsel...

Whenever I picked up a morsel
of bread from the ground I would kiss it
the same with a feather.
My mouth has now become bread for you,
has become a bird...
and the poetry I mouth on the road
but do not write down
will end up as food for the birds.

Rain Fell on the Street after Many Days of Drought...

Rain fell on the street after many days of drought
and lovers in their parked car moved off
revealing the street's privation in dry patches.
The street's allotment of cars is sizeable
like the portion of apples
I buy from the market
wrongly imagining them to be from one tree

An Immense Feeling of Guilt Devours Strangers...

An immense feeling of guilt devours strangers
whenever white cold hunches into their shoulders
as they throw the leftover rice in the trash bins.
I do this a lot, since there's no
hen hut attached to this new house.
And when I threw the rice ball outside
I saw my hands' shadows on the snow
like two crows gathering round
devouring it.

We Erase With the Angles...

We erase with the angles
of the eraser, not with its edges

Like a square eraser
I diminish from my angles and sides
so as to become a perfect circle
merrily rolling across the page

ZIAD ABDELKADER

Translated by Golan Haji and Stephen Watts

In The Mirror Of Andrei Tarkovsky / Native Americans 1819

In the Name of the Lord I lie at rest:
my hands tied behind my back
my head a full metre's distance from my body.
O my brother, my death
would have been more beautiful had we met
in a place other than this eastern world;
in a forest beyond good and evil.

So imagine: I would have
been an antelope slowly wandering through
immense woodlands misted by the breath of trees,
and when I was felled by your arrow
I'd just have managed to see you
standing there in utmost piety,
lowering your head,
hiding your bow behind your back.
And instead of victory yelps,
as if we were enemies,
you would have read beside my head
the native prayer to the antelopes and gazelles:
'We're sorry we killed you,
we respect your courage,
we respect your agility
and your force.'

In The Mirror Of Andrei Tarkovsky / Anton Chekhov 1819

To love a non-existent woman
is no less painful than loving a woman
of flesh and blood.
As for myself I've already fallen for one
    of Chekhov's heroines,
who was lonely enough to allow me
to smooth her bed made by two boards
of yellow pine,
as poor as all of Anton's luckless heroines,
whereas the book that narrates her destiny
is sold in the bookshops like candy.
Every time I keep reading to her
facing her cold bed
until her slow breathing can be heard.
Then I rise, crossing that horrible metaphor
from the head of the page to its foot
pick from the floor her threadbare duvet
and kiss her fevered brow
before closing the book like someone
turning off the light.

AMEER ALHUSSEIN

Translated by Golan Haji and Stephen Watts

The Curtain

In the theatre
everything is possible...
but they didn't tell me that
I would be, solo me, the whole play.
and I forgot it – my blind self
in all the characters;
in a rose
in a thorn
in a watch
in darkness
in a spotlight
in a vacant seat
in the eye of a child
who believed the vicious wolf
and took the meek lamb for a liar.

I saw myself as sniper
kneeling on the roof tops
training my right or left eye slowly...
smoking, I don't know what
then choosing the victim
according to allure
and appearance.

And I saw myself as that victim overwhelmed by life...
moaning, crying out in the streets
riding out dreams
trampling years of ashes.

I am a watch choked by time
on the wrist of a lost and forgotten corpse...
decomposing quietly and returning to first dreams.

I am a ring of silver
or of gold
that was the gift of a beautiful beloved
or a beautiful sister
or of a mother who had the loveliest of faces...
Yes,
or of an elderly father
who pleads with the wolf for his far-off Yusuf...
pleads that the world take care of him.

I am that blue corpse
whose sutures unravelled little by little
to reveal a sky of timbers
not stacked away by friends;
they freed themselves from its burden...
this sky full of black holes –
imprisoning its murderers in eternal nightmares.

I am a kidney stolen from a corpse
implanted in someone else's body...
as if he, I mean the victim,
had only died a little...
just like that;
and somewhere else
your blood keeps pumping
you who were murdered.

....

I am my other stained by my othered blood.
And whenever a phantom jumped out beside me, I said –
while stars romped through my blood – this is me.
How many times I will be disappointed
and then will fall far
into
the void...

As if I was Sisyphus
damned by tiny dreams.
Such rock,
that immense sky.

....

There's still a child
in the country
thinking good of all flowers.
He will say: mother
I touched only the roses.
I, that child who was poisoned;
not believing that beauty can hold poison.

I will not kill the dragonfly...
I will no longer love the praying mantis,
my father.

I am that child who
refused superstition;
not believing that
the devil has a kite called dragonfly.

In the theatre
everything is possible
and what fits me from now on
is only the role of the curtain.

REBER YOUSSEF

Translated by Golan Haji and Stephen Watts

Bombardment Moving From One Branch To Another

'Let my hand be a cure',
my grandmother says at the moment of earth quake
while passing her hand over the ground.
Bomb blasts stroke my shoulder, through a gleam
mirrored by the stainless glass of the window.
what's seen
is deleted by the eye.
Time will not reveal what has been dictated to it.

◆

A brass tap, inside the bus that moves between villages
dried sweat around its handle.
There's a family living on its roof, with a barrel of water.
Slowly the bus moves amid the bomb blasts.
The wheat season rearranges chaotic sentences
in the passengers' conversations

◆

Swiftly the ewes descend the hill toward the water troughs.
The little girl throws the bucket down the well,
distracted by the flower patterns of her dress...
From a nearby leaf of grass, bomb blasts

snake their way through toward her thighs.
Her mother's reiterated calls cannot calm
the circles of water inside the well.

◆

For now I have no secret to reveal to the flower beside me.
Mounting their bicycles, clouds ride over the roofs of mud houses.
It's not bombardment that's falling from my eyes,
with tiny tongues, the sparrows flood the large mud
houses with their singing.

◆

Eavesdropping the summer season, they pass
the great cauldron and matches among themselves,
the women of our neighbourhood, boiling wheat all
night long, the fire in the long street fed by forbidden
books and car tyres worn down by the pathways
of our anti-racist fields.
The horizon catches a murmur, falling from
the narrative of the sky.

◆

My grandmother had no Arabic other than
the opening *sura* and two small sentences she used for her prayer,
and a conversation in the form of a myth –
she, a child of illusion shackled by religion. A conversation between
Munkar and Nakir and those going down to their graves:

'Who is your God?'
'My God is your God.'

Light was trembling on her lips, so the white bird
in her mouth did not become my portion.

She's my book that's opened in my mind forever.
My eye was quick in catching the narrative of light,
during her mumblings that confused the natural cycle
of my in-breath and out-breath,
as if she were about to endure a harsh examination, repeating:
'Who is your God? / My God is your God.'
I failed to kill the monster of doctrine which dwells in her mind,
but she always kicked her words back to my face:
'The Arabic language is the official language of graves in Islam.'
In her youth she had confronted some thieves
who had descended from the mirage to her house
at the end of the road which leads to the village,
she fired a bullet in the air, from the lung of her gun.

NOTE: in Islamic eschatology, Munkar and Nakir are angels who test
the faith of the dead in their graves.

CIWAN QADO

Translated by Golan Haji and Stephen Watts

Nothing Made it Worth the Bother of Opening My Eyes...

Nothing made it worth the bother of opening my eyes
so early in the morning
to take leave of the warm, quiet bed.
All through the night I was reading the Holy Book, I found
nothing sacred there, barring the names of trees and of beasts.
All through the night rain had been falling from heaven and earth
I know my leaving the house won't make the sky hold back its blessing
nor will people become tired of weaving their endless babble.
No one outside thinks of the strange silent grass growing from mud walls.
Everything in this eternal journey of repetitions has remained stagnant,
and no one has glimpsed his own face in the rainwater that's accumulated
                                        in the hoof-print of a lamb.
Nor on the festive day of slaughter do the gentle eyes of the fattened beasts
                                shape themselves in anyone's mind.
So, why
should I leave the house and break the fasts of my mind?
Why should I exchange this generous half-sleep for miser wakefulness?
Everything in this bed's filled with the Simurgh's feathers,
fashioned by the silver knitting needles of skilful women,
and here I become the fertiliser of my shameful secrets
ashes and fuel for my guilt
blue-eyed amulet for my panic.
In the crumpled heart of this bed I dreamt I was dreaming
next to my head the bow and arrow of Boghé Briva go to rust,
the wild rose on my pillow stains my face.

My face is a cold solitary garden
regret has scattered every last one of its roses
over the grave of my gluttonous mind.

NOTE: Boghé Briva is a legendary figure in the Kurdish region
of Syria.

The Moon Would Have Been More Beautiful...

The moon would have been more beautiful
if children could have played marbles on its surface.
Then their shaggy hair full of the shine of moon dust
would have become lanterns for certitude.
But the only perfection
is in loss.
The shed eyelashes of friends
are kept as pledges in their mothers' wall hangings.
I colour the apogee of my rage with henna left
by the hair of spinsters and moustaches of bandits,
while our dying luck is covered with prickly yellow.
In the imagination of every penitent
there's a vicious, nocturnal assassin,
brother to those he wished well but has murdered.
He lathes them with metaphor water, trimming
their sideburns and smoothing slicks off their foreheads
and lays them out in stripy crimson pyjamas
on the flowering wilderness that bursts into bloom

above the beds of the guests.
If it were my call, I would run wild,
alone and naked into the fields,
and lie down under a sycamore tree.
Where I would turn my back on the world
and my face toward pain, the pain that
recites a cradle song to serenity
in lulled tones inside me.

I Never Find Myself Alone...

I never find myself alone
inside me the docile eyes of beasts
submerged in pain and tears follow me,
and I can neither hide from them
nor gaze into their eyes.
With their cold, intense tears
I bathe my wound-encrusted insides
bucket on bucket pouring through me,
with them I expel my fierce blood;
my soul is refreshed
my doubts sluiced.
the tears of beasts
become my blood.

The Stork That Flew Off...

The stork that flew off
from wailing and keen-song
lays its eggs in your
insomniac eyes.
Slowly does it,
stork,
you don't need twigs,
from the outset regret has been preparing
your nest with sticks of cinnamon
broken off by tainted eyes.

MONA KAREEM

Translated by Robin Moger

The poems here are from Kareem's third collection, her first for a full twelve years and the first place I read her poetry at length. It is immediately and evidently poetry engaged with the poet's place in the world, restlessly working its muscles against the weight of language and form and geography. Though far from being purely reactive or descriptive it seems to want to write itself into the possibility of something beyond these deadening inheritances: 'Words need someone | to scrub them with soap, | need looser clothes | and a stranger who won't demand they smile.'

The presence of the casual authority of learned behaviours and expectation, and sometimes the embodied mechanisms of family, country, religion and the city, is the dead soil which Kareem turns and brings spikily alive. Cairo's rain is 'spit' but still she dances in it; the sense is of a metaphor inverted: the spit is real, it is the poem which remakes it as rain. Even the heavy despondency of 'Memories' points to renewal: everything can be thrown off in an instant for all that the struggle is never done.

The jagged imagery of her poems shears and shapes against deadening accumulation. So much is so passionately invested in the poem's ability to open possibilities, to walk us away from the paths laid out, even to resist the possibility of being placed within poetry or as a poet. 'I worry that the question of place will overwhelm every part of myself and reduce me to a one-dimensional person,' Kareem has written. 'In this new collection I wanted to establish a subjective praxis for my poetry for myself that had the capability of extending into future writings.'

A Poet

for Etel Adnan

She wrote a poem about her love
and left it on the balcony.
Her lover came and stole it.

So very alone and so
she always tries to write
about imaginary friends
requesting a poem in exchange
for an invitation to supper.

She dragged her dreams over the page
one after the other
then went to suicide.

One time she neglected her lovers
at the bottom of a notebook: random
bullets killed them.

Memories

A long time since I cut my hair,
a year exactly.
My memory is swollen now,
its weight exhausts my head.

The Room of Darkness

la nuit seule dans ma voix
— *Jean Senac*

I am from darkness, my
homeland is an aging butterfly
my prayers are the desert.

◆

I wash in rain's spit,
in my prayers the sun
dances tip-toe.

◆

My god on the brink of a death.
He the echo's infra-violet.
He is a storm
that loves to talk.

◆

I was born with a genetic defect,
one of twins: I
and solitude.
I shall gift you all a sad heart,
a burst eye, a foot
with twenty toes
and other limbs left me
by my friend Time.

◆

My father budded between sheets
of pouring rain, between
two moments of silence
from the widowed sky.

When I accepted him as a father
he made me paper angels
that I can beat easy
at hide-and-seek.

◆

My father was the first volcano on earth
and our balcony axis of the swirling rain
at the beginning of a feast day.
Our balcony was a rowboat of tears
sometimes sunk in childish clamour.
Our balcony: a life that left the city
and settled in a tub of imagination
...

...
In our new home
there is no balcony

◆

I saw new accessories
worn by the earth
and I saw houses shed their doors
to disassociate themselves
from loved ones parting.

◆

I saw cities abandon their inhabitants,
the train lines creaking
on their back
and weeping the river to bid farewell.

◆

I feel blood vagrant
in my veins
I feel washrooms playing cards
atop my lighthouse head.

◆

Words need someone
to scrub them with soap,
need looser clothes
and a stranger who won't demand they smile.

◆

In light
I see the darkness
I see my god
I see time
I see you
...
...

Threads of Night

Whenever he read a mindless book
his head filled with smoke
and he would search for a bar
to gather the streets
and shadows

Perhaps
you might take God's corpse for your shade
Perhaps
we shall hook our silly homelands
for buttons on the universe's shirt

ALICE GUTHRIE AND MONA KAREEM

The Great Spirits of Translation: a conversation

Alice Guthrie, Shubbak Festival Literary Producer and Arabic translator, is in conversation here with activist and poet Mona Kareem, who has led a campaign to free Ashraf Fayadh. Fayadh, a Palestinian-born poet and curator was sentenced to death in Saudia Arabia in 2015 for renouncing Islam. His sentence provoked an outcry and hundreds of writers and many human rights organisations around the world have campaigned for his release. His sentence was later commuted to lengthy imprisonment and flogging and the campaigning for his release has continued. Mona translated Instructions Within, *the 2008 poetry collection that led to his conviction for apostasy.*

ALICE GUTHRIE: I want to start by asking you about what I see as your poetic activism, or your activist translation (maybe saying how you define it, as a side note, would also be interesting). I'm thinking of course of your work translating Ashraf Fayadh's *Instructions Within*, and on Ashraf Fayadh in general. I wonder if you could give us a bit of background about how you came to be involved in his case, and what the process of translating his work has been like. I know you are keen to spread the word about him and I would really like to hear about your work process on this – partly as it must be so emotionally intense working on this stuff. And I guess connected to that is the question of what else you do that feels linked to this – perhaps all your writing, perhaps your non-literary activism, perhaps something else entirely.

MONA KAREEM: Yes, it is through the advocacy work for Ashraf Fayadh that I fully realized the political role translation plays. Having grown up a monolingual yet devoted reader of world literature, I always understood that literary translation was a revolutionary art. Translation is necessarily subversive and unsettling. Whilst in high school, I used literary translation as a tool to learn English. I would try to translate D. H. Lawrence's

Women in Love line by line. In a way, translation formed my sense of language when using English, as well as my perception and reading of literature. The nurturing side to literary translation became clearer to me when witnessing the collective work done translating Ashraf Fayadh's poetry. I remember back in 2015 when he was awaiting his trial and his case was still pretty unknown I translated a poem that wasn't in *Instructions Within* titled 'Frida Kahlo's Moustache' and I think it is the most translated of his work. It is a love poem, a poem of despair and solitude, and it is written in a destructuralist manner. He writes in 'Frida Kahlo's Moustache':

> Just act as if the earth is silent, as we see it from a distance, and that everything that's happened between us was no more than a bad joke that's gone too far!

I had many translators contacting me, mostly poets, telling me about their translations of Ashraf's work. I realized that, in such moments, we were those strangers that meet quite by chance and become friends. We care about each other, and for each other, with a secret love which binds us. And it was these poets and translators who naturally understood that the best way to support a targeted artist is to engage with his work and bring it forward until he is safe and *here* again.

I have been organizing on behalf of political prisoners in the Arab world for six years now. I simply found my friends were in jail and I had to work with whatever tools I had: talking to writers, artists, translators, activists, organizations, but also writing and translating and being annoying and assertive about it. I know that there are over ten Arab writers still in jail – I am not even familiar with the work of some of them – and often, in the West, the media coverage gives power to the death-bringing nature of regimes, rather than to the resilience and struggle of writers and artists. I see more of us going to jails, I see more of us leaving our home and country, and I think it is inevitable that more collective work must be done in this regard. I look back at the recent history of Latin American writers escaping dictatorships and what their comrades offered them. This comradeship today faces greater challenges as we are living in a hyper-policed world of many borders.

AG: You mention a 'nurturing side' to translation that you witnessed during the collective work on Ashraf's poetry. Could you expand on that idea of 'nurture', and on what that collective work consisted of? And, thinking about all these people, friends of yours or future friends of yours, currently in jail, I want to ask: What form does the collective work that we as readers and writers and translators of poetry can undertake for our kin folk in jail?

MK: Nurturing in the sense that it resembles the patient and tough process of collective organisation. Translation thrives on great spirits – those who are not afraid of getting lost whilst wide awake and absorbed in the creative process. You cannot translate an Arabic poem without knowing Arabic literature, as much as you know the Arabic language. You always have to learn and trace and excavate. And it is always a demanding and long process. So I am not surprised that it is translators (or poets who translate) who have been doing much of the 'hard labour' of translation in Ashraf's case. We are more patient and dynamic than, say, journalists! We sit far away from the sensationalism of media and politics. And I rely on this spirit to keep us working for Ashraf and for other writers and artists, and to find new means of support and solidarity.

AG: I also think it's very interesting that from early on in your life you thought of translation as necessarily subversive and unsettling, as a revolutionary art, no less. I share this view, and it is also what drew me to translation myself; but I find that very often, at least in the literary sphere, translation is instead presented (or perceived) as quite the opposite, really – more of a smooth and invisible means by which the supposed reader can access 'the best in world literature' without any disruption to the commercial notion of the universality of the tale. That's maybe an oversimplification: there is also a notion that translated literature should serve as a sociological document or a piece of ethnography – not that I think that is any less problematic! In reality a great deal of the Arab literature I translate or read (or want to translate or read) is neither universal nor ethnographic, and, when translated, it allows for a radical connection between humans to occur that I find exciting. Is this part of what you mean by the revolutionary art? The 'secret love' you mention here? I ask that because I imagine you also mean something more pragmatic, more concrete, perhaps?

MK: I agree with you that a traditionalist view of translation still dominates, and it is very common amongst translators themselves. How many times have we heard those clichéd metaphors for translation as an 'exchange' or 'bridge'! Or all that talk about how literature, through translation, can bring us together, erase differences, and explain 'misunderstood' cultures such as Arab culture. Within such traditionalist understanding of translation, the most radical act of translation would probably be seen as a betrayal! The translator is always made invisible in the process and asked to act accordingly. Can you leave no trace of you in what you're 'transmitting'? Can you maintain a monogamous relationship with the text? And so on.

In Arabic literature, translation is highly appreciated, sometimes in problematic terms. For classicists, it's blamed and ridiculed as a betrayal of authenticity. Modernists, however, glorify literary translations and would even consider translated literature as the canon on which modern Arabic literature rests. I personally feel most attracted to the playfulness and foreignness of translated texts. Often I read Arabic translations of books I've read in their original language, just to experience the freshness it brings to the contemporary writing medium. I try to camouflage this strangeness in my own writings. I too believe translated poetry is foundational for modern Arabic poetry; however, I don't see the relationship to be one of passive influence. Arabic literary translation has done a spectacular job cannibalizing literatures from English, French, and Spanish. I look at that modernist shift as a rare moment when literature was really concerned and committed to forming an internationalist scene. In my research, I find much joy tracing translations done by Arabic writers. The best of them understood that a good translation is necessarily a contemporary translation. There must be an urgency to a literary translation, a philosophical urgency. And that's quite different from translating a 'relevant work' based on market demand.

I think of translation as a theoretical paradigm; it informs my writing style and continuously challenges essentialist ideas around literature. When I had the opportunity to think about translation in Derridean terms, I felt liberated. I understood that the impossibilities of a text (whether in original or in translation) can be more productive and moving. It allowed me to think about the 'afterlife' of a text, as Walter Benjamin phrases it, and of the new ways I must come up with in order to contribute to the mobility of a chosen text.

AG: I totally agree about the clichés around translation metaphors, although at the same time I guess what some people mean when they talk of a bridge is in fact what I described as the radical connection between humans I mentioned. Maybe it's the magic of translation, the 'secret love' of it that leads to so many overblown metaphors – we're infatuated with it, in some senses, and we can't help ourselves trying to describe it.

I wanted to ask you to expand more about how poetry in Arabic has cannibalised literatures from English, French and Spanish; I think that is something poetry consumers in the Anglosphere know very little about, and it's not something that has gone on in our own literary tradition as such – or at least not so far as we are aware. What form does this take, and what are some of the key examples you have in mind? What is the difference between the way you've seen this happening and the notion of passive influence? And also, is this something of which the ordinary poetry reader in Arabic would be aware?

I'm bearing in mind here that poetry is so much more of a popular genre in the Arabophone world than in the Anglophone one, perhaps more akin to rock music or something, right? So these questions of influence and style are much greater than in our more sheltered niche of Anglophone poetry.

I'd also be interested to hear how this compares with the way that Arabic literary prose relates to translated literature (or literature in other languages) – but that may be another huge topic beyond our scope here.

MK: I came to appreciate the 'cannibalising' nature of Arabic translation through a full revision of Sargon Boulus's translations. Boulus, an Iraqi poet and translator, who went to live in the States, translated over 120 poets, mostly Anglophone and Western, yet not exclusively. Sargon is a prolific translator, but wrote very little as a poet himself – it seems he took all these poets as his own. I thought it was odd that he re-translated Gibran's *Prophet* into Arabic, although there were already at least four translations. Sargon thought none of these translations did an adequate job as they failed to capture the modernist moment in Gibran's text – his stylistic rebellion in writing an early prose poem. Gibran could have written his famous book in Arabic, but there was no precedent for his 'adventure'.

Like Sargon, I've always thought of Walt Whitman as the unofficial father of the Arabic prose poem. Sargon's re-translation of Gibran, a project that he always dreamed of and only completed shortly before his death, aims to restore something missing into its natural context. I found out that Sargon refers to Gibran as the first Arab prose poet in interviews and I then understood a different meaning to what we might call a 'timely translation'. The same is true of his translation of Etel Adnan's poetry: he translated her in a way that makes her an active member of a poetry 'domain' existent at the time. Although not all his translations are successful these two were great works that help us realize that a translation must not be a still corpse or a cold paper in its new home.

I don't think the ordinary Arabic reader is aware of this 'cannibalising' notion and I am not even sure Arab writers would understand my interpretation of these dynamics. I honestly rarely consider the reader in my work! It is a burden to think about someone so anonymous and distant! Poetry is a rich and populist medium in Arabic, yet a rupture was caused by the modern poem. A 'publishable' modern poem is almost by definition in standard Arabic and modernist/post-modernist. And although these poems are the ones that appear in newspapers, get translated and studied, they are still marginal and elitist. Not elitist in a reactionary sense, but because they are examples of a poetry that has had to exist in a 'transnational' way, rather than within the closed domain of a language. I think the post-modernist Arabic poem took this route because it needed to defend and maintain its experimental spirit, which is not necessarily appealing to any reader.

MOHAB NASR

Translated by Robin Moger

More than twenty years passed between the publication of Mohab
Nasr's first collection and his second, during which time the Alexan-
drian poet and writer left Egypt to teach in Kuwait where he has lived
ever since. The poem 'In His Orange Clothes' describes Indian workers
in that country. His return to poetry in 2010 with the publication of
Lord give us a book that we might read, from which three of these poems
come, precipitated an (ongoing) outpouring of poetic production,
much of it released on Facebook or steadily accumulating in files on
his laptop. His departure from Egypt in the wake of personal tragedy
and the suspension of his poetic engagement with all the spaces he was
once a vital part of, permeates his latest work.

My first encounter with Mohab's work came during my translation
of *The Crocodiles*, Youssef Rakha's novel of poetry and political and
personal change in which Mohab's correspondence and poems offer
an intermittent commentary on the failures of passionate engagement
and question the possibility of intellectual sincerity in a society
permeated by opportunism.

The poems included here offer a sense of the gentle lethality of
his approach. Their unabashed lyricism and even romanticism has
a co-opting directness – they are frequently addressed – but this
simplicity is resistant in ways not at first apparent. The imagery, even
the syntax, of these poems is shot through with a dysphoria located in
an insistence on physical distance, the constant failures of linguistic,
emotional and social connection, and again in images of the human
body misfiring and distorted – surprising and *unheimlich*. Returning
to translate the poems I was frequently surprised how difficult it was
to plot the shape of phrases or even to identify the relationship of
verbs with their objects and subjects – his equivocal relationship with
utterance and beauty shaped on the page.

In His Orange Clothes

He ascends
in his orange clothes
from India.
Come here
from Kerala,
from Madras maybe,
with a nod knocked sideways
shakes his head.

They hammer lampposts into this desert and cry
Akash! (Lord of the Sky), Jagdeep! (Light of the Universe)
and do not really mean it.

A small box
bears him up
from the roof of a government truck.

Once more they call:
Akash!
Jagdeep!

From the lip of the box he reached out holding something
and maybe spoke a word
and when he lit the lamp
like him
I saw my country.

A Patch of Light

I have no past only
one of them calls, You!
and I turn
perhaps from weariness,
like someone leant against a lamppost.
I have no future only
one of them calls, You!
and I go forward to put an end
to this charade to leave
an empty patch of light.

My Mother

In place of her thick foot,
her crutch,
and in place of the crutch
her soul would knock the floor
in the room next door
and leave slight grooves.
These I call my life.

The Sea We Know

The sea we know
was a spontaneous motion
a fear running over
holding taut the surface
of our bodies, wave after wave
and time was, too,
a deep blue
in whose depths we tasted
only sand, our hands waving greeting
as though to be saved.
And we would scream sometimes.
But so much water
it would send us back
and we would remain ashore
vomiting up the history of our isolation.
The true sea
the sea we truly feared
was in the sky
was an earth upturned
gazing and saying, Come.
The true sea
spoke just as we did
was defined and clear

beyond bearing

and set stars here and there and sent its silver
oars through the darkness of our souls.

The true sea
was not blind had
no depths even.
It could all be yours
for no more than to think it, at which
you would see the true sea was simple
enough that you could walk with it, so,
hand in hand,
could ask it to directly.
The true sea
did not need your nakedness.
The true sea
was here
when we had it in us, you and I
to love, truly
not understanding what this word might mean.

FADWA SOULEIMAN

Translated by Marilyn Hacker

Fadwa Souleiman (b.1973) was a successful and appreciated actor in
theatre and film in Syria before the revolution. She left her career and
family to join the democratic uprising and became a kind of icon
– addressing the crowds in Homs and leading them in the chant 'One,
One, the Syrian people are one!' – but she was also an eloquent
spokesperson for a nonviolent revolution, interviewed by Egyptian or
Jordanian television and newspapers (there are innumerable YouTube
clips of her in Syria and afterwards). It became more and more
difficult to hold to her positions and she was also from an Alawite
family that disowned her.

She left Syria in 2012 and she is now a political exile in France.
Her first book of poems was published in Beirut in 2013 and the
title translates 'As the moon rises'. It was published in French
translation (translated by Nabil El Azan) in 2014, as *À la pleine lune*.
The following poems are taken from this collection. She continues to
write, poetry, film scripts and other texts, and to reconstruct her life
in Europe.

I knew Fadwa first as a political icon and then as a friend. I
worked with her learning to recite Arabic poetry, Darwish especially,
the way she had in drama school in Damascus, and she wrote an
article about our friendship for *An-Nahar*. I was delighted when
she gave me her collection in Arabic. It seemed like reciprocity to
translate some of these poems. I worked with a bilingual dictionary,
and would go over the translations with another bilingual Syrian
friend to catch errors or references I might have missed.

For Lana Sadiq

On her face, all exiles,
all the roads opened to refugees.
Her face is an olive grove in Haifa and an orange orchard in Jaffa
and West Bank fig trees, and prickly pears from Galilee.
The dove lives in her eyes with the flash of stones thrown by children.
On her lips, the smile of the first daisy opening on the foothills,
and the first tent pitched for refugees, and the first orange dried out
    by bullets
and the first anemones budding
on bodies of the first butterflies fallen to earth here, south of us.
In exile, she searches for her children, to bring them back to her.
I didn't say to her: I am like you, a mother too, at the impossible
    road's beginning
Like you, I'll pace those paths, back and forth, to find my children.
Perhaps one day we'll return together.
And what have I gained, and what have I lost?
And what have I done, Father? My brothers don't love me
And don't want me among them.
What victory there for us, what victory for them?

NOTE: Lana Sadiq is a Palestinian activist.

Image

Within me, a butterfly's strength
and a bull's weakness
I have the mountains' joy
and a spider-web's solidity
the din of ants' feet
and the sea's silence
I have the death-in-life in a cocoon
and the life-in-death of passers-by
the green of autumn leaves
and the grass gone yellow in March
and I have July, the month of Tammuz
who will not return in July
among the days, within me, that moment
when the heart claims its eternal rest
so that everything ends
and there begins within me
what has not yet begun
to begin

When the Moon is Full

Take off your clothes
Rest in the moon
Like a hunger for pomegranates in April
Take off your sorrows and lie down
In night's hammock hung between two stars
Take off your clothes
Wash yourself with the light
And for the light
A breeze has come from the south
Nothing more than a breeze will come from the south
To make fruit trees
Disperse their pollen.

Don't be afraid
Take off your faces
In the calm of night
And let that moon
Unite with you
Oh ball of light
Without fire!
Invite the stars gleaming with grace
As they recite the seasons
Whose canticles blocked
The path of day
So that they can reach you
Open your eyes
Why don't you see the sun?
Move your naked body forward

Standing tall
To pluck off the last leaves
And grasp a skein of sunlight
Enter it
And travel in it
Like an arrow of love
Inhabit the walls of its heart
Like peace
Bring the cold there
Then
Lightning, then thunder.
Don't be afraid
In your right hand, hold
The colour of the tribes, not of bombs
And tint your left hand
With the colour of an oak-tree in April
And the colour of dawn
So that you can cross over
For if you have crossed
So have we all

HISHAM BUSTANI

Translated by Thoraya El-Rayyes

Few poems better capture the cynicism of the infamously irate Hisham Bustani than these two odes to frustration. A poet, short-story writer, political commentator and veteran rabble rouser, Bustani's eventful public life has been punctuated by various brushes with the police state – from harassment by the censors and security services, to arrests for his writing and involvement in political protest.

Bustani's poem 'On the Brink Of' revolves around vivid imagery from the urban landscape of the Jordanian capital Amman, where he lives. Through this imagery, the poem constructs a noisy microcosm of Middle Eastern post-colonial modernity in all its dysfunction – from urban sheep-herding to petrodollar-fuelled sex tourism.

The other poem presented here, 'The Struggle', is a forceful portrait depicting the futility of individual human endeavour in the face of larger forces that shape our world. It conveys an experience of powerlessness no doubt familiar to an author from the would-be revolutionary generation of the Arab Spring, a generation whose years of protest and mobilization eventually proved futile in the face of geopolitical considerations and the power of the deep state.

The Struggle

The world is a punch bag and I, the champion.
I jab with my right,
I weave,
I jab with my left.

I bob to dodge an imaginary opponent whose punches land – wasted
– in the air. My sweat flows heavy, and I exhale – breath after breath
– like a steam train. When my body breaks down and I throw myself
against the wall of the club like a rag, the swinging bag slows little by
little until it stops at exactly the same point where it started: point
zero.

On The Brink Of

Two men carry a palm tree downhill to the end of the street.
Where are you taking your mother, you ingrates?
At the end of the street, a dumpster.
The men walk back, side by side.
One talks into his mobile, the other picks his nose.

A *jilbab*-wearing woman walks along with two girls.
One holds onto the edge of the long, button-down cloak, tripping as
she walks but never letting go.
The other: as soon as her mother throws away an empty juice box, she
jumps onto it – keeps jumping and jumping. There is an ancient
bloodfeud between them.
The box has become part of the street, and she is still jumping.
And the *jilbab*-wearing woman and her stumbling hanger-on have
disappeared from the scene.

Many cars drive by.
Some speed up as they turn into the street, letting out the screech of
tyres and roar of the engine.

Others are slow.
If I hadn't been watching I wouldn't have noticed them pass.

An elegant young man in shiny sunglasses hurries past, glancing at his mobile every three steps. Maybe he is late for a date with her.

IF YOU HAVE WASHING MACHINES, TABLES TAPS IRON PIPES, WATER TANKS, FRIDGES, COUCHES, BATTERIES, FOR SAAAAAAALE.
The small junk truck passes by with a boy hanging out the side, his eyes scanning the neighbourhood windows.
The morning is hot, and the air is heavy, and nothing moves. No one wants to sell their junk and furniture today.

More *jilbab*ed women and small children.
A huge stream of *jilbab*ed women and small children walk up the hill.
At the top of the hill – out of sight – is the mosque charity centre.

The sound of lewd laughter.
At high noon, women of the night step out of a car with a Saudi plate and the street trembles from the blows of their sharp, high heels.

The morning call to prayer.
The morning call to prayer again, with a slight difference: 'Prayer is better than sleep' it announces.
The midday call to prayer.
The iqama calls out: 'Prayer has commenced'.
The entire Eid service from prayer call to culmination.

Young men on horses ride along the street, back and forth.
A flock of sheep amble along swaying to the rhythm of the bellwether

and 'Hshhhshhhh, hshhhhhhh' their shepherd shoos them away from sidewalk trees and neighbourhood gardens.
When his voice doesn't reach one, a pebble flying out of his hand will.

Is *this* a city?

A light breeze enters the window and the curtain moves a little.
From behind it, you can see the *jilbab*ed women, as if a factory at the beginning of the street keeps churning them out.

A car selling just-sliced watermelons calls out.
A car selling potatoes and green peppers and cauliflower.
The candyfloss seller dispenses the squeal of his plastic whistle.
The corn-on-the-cob man yells 'CORRRRRRRRRN' drawing it out so that it stretches from the beginning of the street to the end of it. It would not fit on this page.

There are ants on the kitchen table. Small blond ants. There is a spider who has woven a web in the corner of the shower. A cockroach appears every now and then in the bathtub but does not survive long, before being battered with a squeegee mop.

I feel a tingle on my body and violently smack it in the hope of killing the insect crawling there – between the hairs – trying to wake me.
Maybe it's just a breeze coming in from the window, tickling the hairs.
Maybe it is my brain being tickled. But I smack anyway, then the tingle reappears elsewhere. And I smack.

I grind my teeth. I know I do it because my teeth hurt, so I relax my jaw. I stay that way: on the brink of consciousness, the brink of sleep, the brink of anxiety.

Air does not enter my nostrils. The sounds get louder and intertwine into a chaotic clamour. Tens of disorderly ping pong balls fall, bouncing off the walls of my skull.

It's time to wake up.

I look at the time first: 11.23am. Then I see them in my room: the *jilbab*ed women, the children, the corn-on-the-cob seller, the junk truck, the two mother-murdering men with the palm tree, the flock of sheep, the small blond ants, the prostitutes, the speeding cars and those quietly driving by, the worshippers, and the headache.

'Why do you sleep so late?' asks a woman who disappears behind black clothing and continues on her way without awaiting an answer. 'Why do you sleep naked?' asks the small boy hanging out the side of the junk truck.

'What is this strange plaster on your nose?' asks the prostitute.

The ants quietly climb the bed.

I close my eyes and draw in a breath... two breaths. And when I open them, the first thing I see is the time: 12:09pm. They have all left. All of them except the headache. And the noise coming in from the window does not stop.

I take a quick shower. I put on my clothes. Four sprays of cologne. As I turn on the ignition, the sound of a rock band comes out of the speakers – Dave Grohl's loud yell 'Who are you?' And I drive off.

The sound of guitars and accordions piles onto the loose mass of noise coming from outside. I raise my head and watch my car pass slowly by, with me behind the wheel wearing sunglasses and banging my head to the rhythm as I disappear behind a street corner.

'Wind me up and watch me spin'

'Watch me spin'

'Watch me spin'

More *jilbab*ed women. More cars. Not the sound of a single bird.

The time? The time is 1:16pm.

I close my eyes.

I see two men carrying a palm tree downhill to the end of the street.

Where are you taking your mother, you ingrates?

NAJWAN DARWISH

Translated by Kareem James Abu-Zeid

Born in Jerusalem in 1978, Najwan Darwish is one of the foremost
Palestinian poets of the twenty-first century. His poetry has won acclaim
in the Arab world and abroad for its wide-ranging aesthetics, being both
specifically Palestinian and global in its scope. His use of irony and
humour, for example, represent a significant departure from the strains
of heroic and declamatory Arabic poetry of the second half of the
twentieth century. Although much of his work conveys a spirit of
resistance (resistance to the Occupation of Palestine, resistance to
oppression in all its forms, resistance to fundamentalism, resistance to
authoritarianism...), the political is just one of its many layers. The lucid
poetic subject of this verse is not immune to its own critiques, and the
highbrow heroic tone of past Palestinian verse is countered here with
Darwish's down-to-earth poetics and gritty explorations of the human
psyche. No, this poetry does not shy away from the harsh realities of life
in Palestine and the modern Arab world, but neither does it ever fully
give up hope – this, perhaps, is its greatest act of resistance.

The Master Is Disappointed in His Disciple

As I was emerging from beneath the rubble
I caught a glimpse of you
leaving with the traitors:
You weren't in one of the First Class seats.

Even in betrayal
you couldn't make the grade.

The Ruins of Our Families

I don't have a widow who'll be there
on the night of my commemoration
to receive the poet's coat of arms
and dole out downcast smiles –
any melancholic woman
can be my widow then.

I have no offspring either –
the children born amid the shelling
in these sullen hospitals
are simply companions:
they're joining this family
we've created from the ruins of our families.

A thousand years might pass
but still I won't be a father.
I'll stay where I am,
I'll remain
one of the youngest, most reckless
of these children
(but that won't stop them
from taking me for their father).

I'll fight to the bitter end
for the right
not to be a father
to my children.

How Many?

How many bedrooms do I need
to get a bit of sleep?
How many chairs
to sit myself down?
How many roads
to walk back to you,
my distant country?
This time I've gone
and I'm not coming back.
Your job, now, is to slip out,
lovesick and afraid,
and come in search of me.

Little Malta

The fog this morning is four thousand years old,
as is that woman passing beneath my window.

A little while ago
I stood in fog just like this
and saw a woman just like that
while my peers, laughing like real pirates,
hid plundered ships in our small bay,
for Haifa was coming to be called Little Malta....
You kind-hearted pirates whose greatest ambition is to please a woman,
whose greatest hope is a night when the lanterns are lit and the glasses
        are filled,

you pirates for whom the sea is the lover of your mother, the land,
and life the wife of your father, death –
in a little while
empires will crash into each other like aging ships;
in a little while
invaders will land here, disguised as refugees;
in a little while
oblivion will descend like the fog at dawn
and swallow your voices and gestures and ropes;
in a little while
the pirates of cement mixers and atom bombs
will land.

But I can make out your laughter amid this fog
while you return in plundered ships,
your greatest hope to please a woman....
Which one of you took my glass from the table?
Which one of you is drinking it now
and laughing
as you whisper the words
'To your health'?

NOTE: 'Little Malta' was a nickname for Haifa in the seventeenth and
eighteenth centuries, when the city briefly rivalled Malta as a haven for
pirates and a harbour for stolen ships.

A Story about the Closing of the Sea

When you turn down that street at the city's edge,
the one that leads to the camp,
if you see children leaving that school that resembles a prison,
if you see seven of them standing there, on the threshold of silence,
    and watching,
if you see a raw-boned child whose eyes are gleaming with all the
    world's promises,
you'll have found my friend Tayseer.
His family has a country that was stolen in broad daylight,
and you can see the birds waking in his worried eyes,
and cement houses,
and memories of tin sheets,
and voices that were fearful
of the occupying army's transceivers
throughout the long weeks of curfew.
But none of this has taken the slightest spark from his eyes:
he saw the sea once, and nothing can convince him
that he won't see it again.
'When the curfew's lifted, we'll take you to the sea' –
that's how they used to comfort him.
And when the curfew finally *was* lifted one evening, they said,
'The sea's closed now, go to sleep.'
He didn't sleep that night – he imagined an old man
who closed the sea by lowering a massive tin sheet that stretched from
    the star on the horizon to the sand on the shore;
the man secured it with a huge padlock (larger than the one on
    Tayseer's father's shop on Omar Mukhtar Street),
then went back to his home.

When you walk down that street at the city's edge,
the one that leads to the camp,
if you see two eyes gleaming with all the world's promises,
ask them, I beg you, if the Gaza Sea has opened yet,
or if it's still closed.

Translated by the author

I'm fascinated by Sumerian clay tablets and by the symbols and images inscribed on them; not only because they were the first recorded communication in history but also because they were poetic by default: they were the metaphors of things and not the things themselves. But they gradually lost their poetic features as they developed into modern languages. The tablets are our Iraqi Haiku, if you will.

In my book *The Iraqi Nights* I tried to imitate those ancient tablets by making drawings in their style to accompany my modern short sections of poetry. It helped a lot that I was a terrible artist because the images are supposed to be primitive. I continued writing tablets. Now I have 99 of them and I am going to stop because I am scared of the number 100 for some reason.

Tablets III

1

Like the turtle,
I walk everywhere
with my home on my back.

2

The mirror on the wall
doesn't show any of the faces
that used to pass
in front of it.

3

The dead
act like the moon:
they leave the earth behind
and move away.

4

Oh, little ants,
how you move forward
without looking back.
If I could only borrow your steps
for five minutes.

5

All of us are autumn leaves
ready to fall at any time.

6

The spider makes a home outside itself.
It doesn't call it exile.

7

Forgotten
the faces of the dead
as if we met them once
through revolving doors.

8

I am not a pigeon
to know my way home.

9

Just like that,
they packed our green years
to feed a hungry sheep.

10

Of course you can't see the word love.
I wrote it on water.

11

When the moon is full
it looks like a zero.
Life is round
at the end.

12

The grandfather left the country with one suitcase.
The father left with empty hands.
The son left with no hands.

13

No, I am not bored of you.
The moon, too, comes every day.

14

She drew her pain:
a colourful stone
settled deep inside the sea.
The fish pass it by,
they can't touch it.

15

She was safe
inside her mother's belly.

16

The lanterns know the value of night
and they are more patient
than the stars.
They stay until morning.

17

Those colourful flowers
over the mass graves
are the dead's last words.

18

The Earth is so simple,
you can explain it with a tear or a laugh.
The Earth is so complicated,
you need a tear or a laugh
in order to explain it.

19

The number you see now
will inevitably change
with the next dice roll.
Life won't show its faces
all at once.

20

I love you
as a singular
even though I use the plural,
both the regular and irregular plurals.

21

The sweet moment is over.
I spent an hour
thinking of that moment.

22

The butterfly brings pollen,
with its little feet, and flies away.
The flower can't follow it.
Therefore its leaves flutter,
and its crown is wet
with tears.

23

Some of our tribal members
died in war.
Some died regular deaths.
None of them died from joy.

24

That woman standing in the public square
is made of copper.
She's not for sale.

Eleven Men in a Court of Women

The Midnight Court: Eleven Versions of Merriman, by Gregory A.
Schirmer, Lilliput Press, 2015

Composed sometime in the late eighteenth century and preserved
orally before eventually being written down in 1850, Brian Merriman's
Cúirt an Mheán Oíche, or *The Midnight Court*, is the greatest comic poem
in Irish literature, and certainly one of the most controversial. Sexually
risqué, searingly satirical, feminist, and bravely anti-establishment, the
thousand-line poem has been translated, banned, maligned, lauded
and butchered over the course of the last two centuries.

Borrowing from the *aisling* tradition of Irish-language literature
and song, in which a female embodiment of Éire tells the poet of
Ireland's struggle and its future rejuvenation, Merriman's poem offers
not so much a vision of national hope, but a piercing attack on sexual
impotence and inadequacy. Falling asleep by the banks of a river, the
poet wakes to the sight of a huge, hideous and relatively aggressive
woman, who tells him he has been summoned to a court 'of mercy,
of virtue, and of women'. This court, led by a faery-woman named
Aoibheall, is packed with a host of women 'boiling with every anger',
sick of their mistreatment at the hands of the country's men, who are
by turns accused of erectile dysfunction, celibacy, patriarchal law-
making and the inability to bring women to orgasm.

Interestingly, despite its largely sex-positive emphasis on female
sexuality and its canonical status, there has been no published
translation of *The Midnight Court* by a woman poet. Gregory
Schirmer's new book, *The Midnight Court: Eleven Versions of Merriman*,
looks at eleven translations of the poem, all by men, written between
the early decades of the nineteenth century and 2005. The approach
allows not only a comparative study of different methods of verse

translation, but also an insight into the cultural (and sometimes legal) pressures which shape the act of bringing a poem out of one language and into another, and out of the eighteenth century into the world of the translator. Seamus Heaney, who translated *Cúirt an Mheán Oíche* alongside passages from Ovid in 1993, noted the poem's peculiar ability 'to subsume into itself the social and intellectual preoccupations of different periods'. As Schirmer deftly shows, Merriman's text has been variously used as a vessel for critiques of colonialism, sectarianism, the class system, the Catholic Church, and the act of translation itself.

While the best of Merriman's translators manage to express their own poetic interests within the orbit of the original text, many prioritise the concerns and prejudices of the translator over those of Merriman's original. One of the earlier versions of the poem, put into English by Irish-American Michael O'Shea and given the subtitle 'A Rhythmical Bacchanalia', verges at times on severe misrepresentation of the original, inserting references to 'greedy robbers from a foreign coast', imbuing the eighteenth-century poem with the discourse and language of nineteenth-century Romanticism and nationalism. Other translators, such as Denis Woulfe, sanitised the more frank discussions of sexuality with florid language, cutting out significant chunks of the poem in the process. In fact, *The Midnight Court* is so forthright in its arguments, so dramatic in its structure and so metrically insistent that the voice of the author can be heard echoing through even the most careless or deceptive translation.

The context of colonialism, marginalisation and social upheaval is present throughout, and in many ways the sexual impotency of the accused men is linked to the political impotency of the colonised Irish. There are passages which directly address an Ireland:

> Without property, without freedom for an ancient race,
> Sovereignty in law or rent or rulers,
> The land destroyed and nothing after it

and it is hard not to associate this vision of an oppressed country with the subjected women of the court, who long for equality, passion and justice. It is difficult, reading the poem, to imagine that it was composed in the eighteenth century. *Cúirt an Mheán Oíche* is persistently radical, and calls for a sort of egalitarian society yet to be realised. Take, for example, the passage on the treatment of illegitimate children, celibacy among the clergy, and the supposed sanctity of marriage. The voice of the woman speaker cuts through all established ideas of class, dogma and patriarchy in an overhaul of established norms, asking:

> where is the need for the commotion of the wedding [...]
> since the embryo that the Son of God bestowed ripened
> Without a priest in the world giving them [the parents] to each other

She insists on the unnaturalness of class-based social relations, calling on the court to 'Make free to sleep without a cloak, without fetters | The seed of the churl and of the boastful noble blood'. Schirmer's book includes as an appendix a full printed text of Merriman's poem accompanied by a 'literal' translation, from which I am quoting, but readers of Irish need only read a few lines of the original to understand the ribald force of the metrics and the constant, outrageous, joyous innuendo. Schirmer's book displays a laudable ability to identify and explore the key pressures and symptoms on the act of poetic translation over 200 years of Irish history. It is not only valuable as a critical resource on Merriman's translators, who include Seamus Heaney and Ciarán Carson, but also to anyone interested in translation as both a political and artistic act. Reading Merriman's poem is a revelation, and its feisty, controversial and still radical assertion that 'it's time...to submit to the law of women' has evidently set many a male poet-translator hot under the collar. Most importantly, in the context of this book, *Cúirt an Mheán Oíche* has allowed successive generations of writers to channel the spirit of social ferment throughout modern Irish history, and has been in turn shaped and reimagined under various social and biopolitical pressures. *Eleven Versions of Merriman* offers, at another key juncture in Irish social and sexual history, an opportunity to revisit, to reassess, and to reflect on a poem which has consistently garnered controversy and praise in the most outrageous and unashamed way.

Seán Hewitt

Seeking Poets Along The Songlines

A Little Tour Through European Poetry by John Taylor, Transaction Publishers, 2014

John Taylor's translations of contemporary poetry from Europe travel first class along the personal essays that make this a welcome anthology; it not only matters who you read, but where you read. Out searching for Hölderlin's Tübingen 'We drove back in the opposite direction. The rush-hour traffic was increasing in quantity but not decreasing in speed. There was no comfort "against the chaos of our time"'.

A Little Tour through European Poetry, sequel to *Into the Heart of European Poetry,* is a translator's pilgrimage through over twenty European countries and beyond into Turkey and Russia. The 'Little' of the title pre-empting the inevitable accusations of errors and omissions as no anthology can ever hope to plot the Borgesian all-inclusive map; the Grandest of all Tours that only a Romantic would dream of! But a mapping it is nonetheless, with Taylor at every station to take you by the hand, welcoming you off the train to European poets and their cities.

We meet Klaus Merz 'on the Strassenbahn' in disarmingly sincere mood:

> Since five o'clock it's been raining
> the horizon makes
> no fuss
> about this.
>
> Actually a love poem
> has no need of weather
> Darling.

The themes are as varied as the original languages they are written in. The quotidian of post break-up Yugoslavia; Gottfried Benn's

'Unexpected Compassion'; an Albanian childhood; the Greek War of
Independence, Civil War and Junta and 'A Panorama of Turkish Love
Poetry'. Take for example these two expressions on love, the major
theme of the anthology:

> I touched you. You screamed back hoarsely!
> (you were smoking your cigarette butt on a pin).
> But so was I, you know? Stabbed,
> I didn't even want you forever, just an evening,
> on rent, and barely that.

(by Sandro Penna)

> All relationships
> are long distance
> but I am not
> from here and I leave
> no descendants,
> I want no other origin
> than this bridge
> for as long as it holds.

(by Maria do Cebreiro)

His inclusion of Maria do Cebreiro, along with Vicente Aleixandre
from Spain, are telling examples of Taylor's method: a willingness to
re-engage with an overlooked or too quickly forgotten poet – in this case
Aleixandre, and in an earlier chapter, Gottfried Benn – alongside a new
voice. Do Cebreiro is part of the generation of young Galician poets who
are reshaping the literary mould the Galician, and the Galician woman
in particular, had been forced into since the misreading of Rosalia de

Castro as the hand-wringing, edge-of-the-cliffs stoic victim was set in stone. Do Cebreiro and her contemporaries are doing what Eavan Boland and others did for women poets in Ireland, who as a result can now be simply referred to as poets, (although the Spanish pronoun will always maintain the distinction).

Do Cebreiro's collection *Non so de aquí* (I am not from here), shows her to be an obliquely intimate poet, writing personal poems of alienation and longing that respond to Adam Zagajewski's 'Why is childhood our only origin, our only longing?' as quoted by Taylor. In the sequence of smart and smarting poems from which Taylor selects, Do Cebreiro rejects the inherited role of the Galician woman, imposed, as is so often the case, from within:

A homeland is, like love,
the daughter of absolute misery
and extravagance.

From 'Biscaia (the Law of the Father)'

Do Cebreiro, like all of the selections here, is a welcome choice by Taylor. *A Little Tour of European Poetry* is a primer for readers and translators, a preliminary treatment readying the reader for further soakage in contemporary European poetry. No more than a cosmetic covering perhaps, a glossing over, but enough to pique the reader's attention.

Each meeting adds layers to European poetry and to the very art and fact of poetry translation. Michael Hofmann is considered perhaps 'too inventive,' Jorie Graham's verbose renderings of Patrizia Cavalli are scrutinized and further lexicographical jousting gives the reader a sense of what may befall the translator. Which leads to the one fault with this collection. And that is the absence of the poems in their original language. On the few occasions where we get to see the originals – with

Hofmann and Graham for example – we begin to get a sense of the consequence of translation.

Having the poems in their original one might be tempted to listen out for a 'Songlines' of European poetry, the score sheet of languages from which these poems were first sung into being. It would also be useful to put Taylor's translations, or the translators he has chosen, to the test as he himself does with Hoffman and others. Taylor quotes original lines throughout the anthology to make the point about a linguistic or aural effect, as when talking of Gottfried Benn: 'The German distich 'Ruhe sanft | kleine Aster!' ('Rest easy, | little aster!'), opens with two particularly gentle words, suitable for a lullaby or a reassuring remark to a friend; one even hears a distant echo of the noun 'Ruh' (peace) found in one of Goethe's most famous poems, 'Über allen Gipfeln / ist Ruh' ('Over all the peaks / is peace')'.

Taylor's expertise is obviously not in question, but not quoting the originals keeps the reader at one remove from the poem. And yet for that slight and, it has to be said, single quibble, *A Little Tour* is a thoroughly engaging journey through contemporary European poetry, and John Taylor a trustworthy guide. I hope it won't be long before Taylor gives in to his temptation 'to add a few Irish and English poets to this anthology in order to determine what bridges or underwater tunnels might connect continental poetry to that of Eire and the Isles.' Nuala Ní Dhomhnaill – who lived for a time in Turkey and writes almost exclusively in Irish – comes to mind. As does Michael Hartnett – arguably the most successful translator into English of Lorca's *Romanceros* – as well as a host of young poets in Ireland today writing in Irish. I sense though that it won't be long before Taylor is writing back to us from the ferry to Dun Laoghaire with his 'pickings and choosings' from the shelves of Dublin's bookshops.

Keith Payne

Language of Flint and Tongue of Air

Poems of Osip Mandelstam, selected and translated by Peter France,
New Directions, 2014
Osip Mandelstam: Voronezh Notebooks, translated by Andrew Davis,
NYRB Poets, 2016

Although these volumes present translations of the same poet, they
shouldn't be thought of as being in direct competition. Peter France's
Poems of Osip Mandelstam offers a selection of poems from every stage
of the great Russian's career, from the pre-Revolution poems of *Stone* to
the clandestine 'Moscow' and 'Voronezh Notebooks', as they are known –
sequences written before his arrest by the NKVD and during his sentence
of internal exile, later preserved by his widow Nadezhda. As such,
France enters a crowded field, with similar selections already available
from W.S. Merwin, James Greene, and Christian Wyman, among others.
By contrast, Andrew Davis offers the complete 'Voronezh Notebooks' in
isolation; the only other similar volume is *The Moscow and Voronezh
Notebooks*, translated by Richard and Elizabeth McKane, of which the
kindest thing that can be said is that it provides a wonderful invitation
for those without Russian to attempt their own, aesthetically more
satisfying versions.

This difference between the two volumes has further implications
for how one should appraise them. Having elected to do the 'Voronezh
Notebooks' in their entirety, Davis may be excused if the occasional
poem is more serviceable than inspired; but France has to demonstrate
that his versions are worth reading alongside those by Merwin,
Greene, et al.

W.S. Merwin's versions (made in collaboration with the pathbreaking
Mandelstam scholar Clarence Brown) were the first substantial
translations into English, and they set an odd precedent by rendering

a consistently formal poet in free verse, earning the withering
condemnation of Joseph Brodsky. (Despite that, Merwin's often have
a grace and force later translators have been unable to match.) The
subsequent history of Mandelstam in English has thus been – more
so than with many other foreign-language poets – an attempt to find
closer equivalents for the forms of the originals. Davis and France
both attempt this by using assonance and other techniques where
strict adherence to full rhyme would be impossible. France's greatest
success with this is probably the 'Slate Pencil Ode' from 1923, in
which he sustains alternate rhyme across nine 8-line stanzas without
wrenching the syntax out of joint: it is, I think, the most convincing
version of this poem currently in print.

If Mandelstam's apocalyptic odes of the early 1920s are
long-distance runs, the three sequences that make up the 'Voronezh
Notebooks' are a series of sprints, or imperilled dashes from one bit
of cover to the next. Andrew Davis captures the breathless quality
of these short lyrics, often replicating Mandelstam's punctuation
and abrupt syntax:

> Alone, I look into the face of the cold:
> It—going nowhere; myself—from nowhere
> (from '47')

Compare Peter France's more pedestrian, explicit unpacking
of the same:

> Alone, I look into the frost's face:
> nowhere I came from, it is going nowhere.

But Davis goes further, frequently contracting 'I have to' into the
slangy imperative 'gotta', and a line like 'Smart-ass pimp of water and

wine' ('80') surely carries Mandelstam too far towards the idiom of hip-hop. This handling of Mandelstam is possible with the Voronezh poems, which are more idiosyncratic, with a more heterogeneous range of reference, than his earlier classicising poetry with which France is more at home.

This isn't to say that France is uninspired or risk-averse. In the final stanza of '61' ('Armed with the eyesight of skinny wasps'), for instance, Davis follows the word-order of the Russian quite closely:

> If only I, stalling sleep and death,
> Could somehow, someday catch
> The chirp of the air and summer warmth,
> Hear the slipping earth, the slipping earth...

France's version is metrically much more regular, and he drastically re-orders the clauses to clinch the stanza with a rhyme:

> Oh if I too could one day be impelled
> by summer's heat and by the air's sharp practice
> to feel, as I avoided sleep and death,
> earth's axis, yes, to penetrate earth's axis...

Neither translator can bring over the wordplay on 'os', 'wasps', through which Mandelstam punningly inscribes his own first name and that of his nemesis, Joseph Stalin, in this poem. But Davis compensates with a pun of his own, whereby Mandelstam tries 'stalling' the fate decreed by the one who named himself the 'man of steel'.

It would be unfair, for reasons already discussed, to keep comparing Davis's and France's versions of the later poems to decide which is 'best' – unfair, and beside the point. For anybody wanting to read right through the poems of Mandelstam's last creative period, Andrew

Davis's will now be the go-to edition, while those wanting a fresh (or their first) look at Mandelstam's classic poems will find a great deal to please them in Peter France's. It's only a slight shame that France's substantial volume is presented in a slender, though admittedly well-produced, pamphlet format.

Henry King

NOTES ON CONTRIBUTORS

KAREEM JAMES ABU-ZEID is an award-winning translator of Arabic poetry and prose, including books by Najwan Darwish, Rabee Jaber, and Dunya Mikhail, among others.

PAUL BATCHELOR won the Stephen Spender Prize for Translation in 2009. He teaches English literature and Creative Writing at Durham University.

CELESTIAL BRIZUELA was born in San Salvador de Jujuy, Argentina, in 1984. Her first approach to art was through poetry. She studied screenwriting at the Universidad del Cine in Argentina.

HISHAM BUSTANI is an award-winning author acclaimed for his bold style, unique narrative voice and experiments at the boundaries of short fiction and prose poetry. English-language translations of his work have appeared in literary journals including *World Literature Today*, *The Los Angeles Review of Books* and *3:AM*.

MERCEDES CEBRIÁN is a translator, poet and fiction writer. Her writing has been published in journals newspapers and magazines such as *El País*, *Poetry London* and *Long Poem Magazine*.

LAURA CHALAR (1976) was born in Montevideo, Uruguay, where she trained as a lawyer. She is the author of seven books, most recently *Midnight at the Law Firm* (Coal City Press, 2015), a poetry collection. Laura is also a Pushcart Prize nominee.

NAJWAN DARWISH is an acclaimed Palestinian poet whose work has been translated into over 20 languages, including the English volume *Nothing More to Lose* (NYRB, 2014).

TERENCE DOOLEY's translation of Eduardo Moga's *Selected Poems* has just been published by Shearsman Books, and his own poems, *The Why of it,* recently came out with Argent Press.

WALID EL-MASRI is a Syrian-Lebanese artist who was born in Damascus in 1979. He lives and works in Paris. His paintings have been exhibited worldwide, in solo and group exhibitions. https://walidelmasri.net/

THORAYA EL-RAYYES is a literary translator who specializes in bringing Arabic literature from the Levant into English. Her translations have appeared in literary journals including *World Literature Today*, *The Literary Review*, *The Common* and *Banipal*.

GEORGE GÖMÖRI, poet, critic and scholar, was born in Budapest but, after his involvement in the Hungarian uprising of 1956, went into exile. From 1969 till 2001 he was a Lecturer in Polish and Hungarian at the University of Cambridge. He has published fourteen books of poetry in Hungarian and translated many Hungarian poets into English.

ALICE GUTHRIE is a freelance translator, writer and editor. She is Literary Producer of Shubbak, London's biennial festival of Arab arts and culture.

MARILYN HACKER is the author of thirteen books of poems, most recently *A Stranger's Mirror, New and Selected Poems 1994–2014* (W.W. Norton, 2015), and of sixteen collections of translations from the French. Her translations from Arabic have appeared in *POEM*, *The Wolf*, *AGNI*, *Prairie Schooner* and *The Paris Review*.

GOLAN HAJI is a Syrian Kurdish poet and translator who now lives in Paris. His latest poetry collection, *Scale of Injury*, was published by Al-Mutawassit, Milan, in 2016. *A Tree Whose Name I Don't Know* in Stephen Watts' translation is published by A Midsummer Night's Press. His most recent translation into Arabic is Alberto Manguel's *All Men Are Liars* (Dar al-Saqi, Beirut, 2016).

SEÁN HEWITT won a Northern Writers' Award in 2016. His poetry has been published in POETRY, *The Poetry Review* and *The New Statesman*, amongst others. He is currently a PhD candidate at the Institute of Irish Studies, University of Liverpool.

YOHANNA JARAMILLO was born in Tijuana, Mexico in 1979. Her most recent collection is *32°/33* (Ediciones El Humo, 2014).

ANJA KAMPMANN is a German poet and author of fiction. She was awarded the MDR-Literaturpreis as well as the Wolfgang-Weyrauch-Förderpreis. Her first collection of poetry was published by Carl Hanser Verlag, 2016. She lives in Leipzig.

MONA KAREEM is a poet-writer-translator based in New York. She is the author of three poetry collections. Her translations include Ashraf Fayadh's *Instructions Within* and an Arabic selection of Alejandra Pizarnik's poems.

J. KATES is a poet and literary translator who lives in Fitzwilliam, New Hampshire.

BAKHYT KENJEEV was born in Chimkent, Kazakhstan in 1950. His youth was spent in Moscow, and he began writing poetry in Russian at 18. His first collection of poems lay buried in the archives of Kazakhstan Writer's Union for 20 years. It was finally published in his country of birth in 1996. Kenjeev is now a citizen of Canada who lives in New York.

HENRY KING teaches at Malmö University, Sweden. His versions of Osip Mandelstam have appeared in *MPT* and *Stand*.

LIANG YUJING is the Chinese translator of *Best New Zealand Poems 2014*. His forthcoming books of translation include *What Do Women Want: Poems by Kim Addonizio* (in China) and *Zero Distance: New Poetry from China* (Tinfish Press, USA).

CRÌSDEAN MACILLEBHÀIN (Christopher Whyte) is the author of five collections of poetry, four novels in English, and translations from the work of European poets including Pasolini, Rilke and Tsvetaeva. Born in Glasgow in 1952, he has spent many years living and writing in mainland Europe. He currently divides his time between Budapest and Trieste.

DAVID MCKAY's recent literary translations include *War and Turpentine* by Stefan Hertmans and Multatuli's classic *Max Havelaar* (a joint translation with Ina Rilke, to be published in 2018). He hopes to find a publisher for an English edition of the complete published poems of Vasalis.

DUNYA MIKHAIL was born in Iraq and left for the United States in 1996. Her books include *The Iraqi Nights, Diary of A Wave Outside the Sea*, and *The War Works Hard*. She also edited a pamphlet of Iraqi poetry titled *15 Iraqi Poets*. She was awarded the Kresge Fellowship, Arab American Book Award, and UN Human Rights Award for Freedom of Writing.

ROBIN MOGER is a freelance translator of Arabic with a particular interest in twentieth-century and contemporary prose and poetry.

KATRINA NAOMI's most recent collection is *The Way the Crocodile Taught Me* (Seren, 2016).

MOHAB NASR is a poet and writer and a journalist for the Kuwaiti newspaper *Al-Qabas*. He has published two collections of poetry, *That a bird steal your eyes* and *Lord, give us a book that we might read* and has been involved in founding and contributing to two influential literary magazines both from Alexandria, *Al Arba'iyoun* (The Wednesdayists) and *Amkina* (Places).

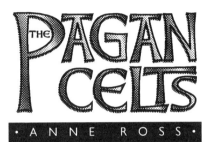

THE PAGAN CELTS

·ANNE ROSS·

Fighting Gaul, with horned helmet, torc, belt and, originally,
a spear. Probably late 3rd century BC